DEEPENING Digital ››››› Citizenship

A Guide to Systemwide Policy and Practice

**Carrie Rogers-Whitehead
AND Vanessa Monterosa**

PORTLAND, OREGON • ARLINGTON, VIRGINIA

Deepening Digital Citizenship

A Guide to Systemwide Policy and Practice
Carrie Rogers-Whitehead and Vanessa Monterosa

© 2023 International Society for Technology in Education

World rights reserved. No part of this book may be reproduced or transmitted in any form or by any means—electronic, mechanical, photocopying, recording, or by any information storage or retrieval system—without prior written permission from the publisher. Email permissions@iste.org for more information.

Library of Congress Cataloging-in-Publication Data

Names: Rogers-Whitehead, Carrie, 1983- author. | Monterosa, Vanessa, author.
Title: Deepening digital citizenship : a guide to systemwide policy and practice / Carrie Rogers-Whitehead and Vanessa Monterosa.
Description: First Edition. | Portland, Oregon : International Society for Technology in Education, [2023] | Includes bibliographical references and index.
Identifiers: LCCN 2022050362 (print) | LCCN 2022050363 (ebook) | ISBN 9781564849663 (Paperback) | ISBN 9781564849670 (epub) | ISBN 9781564849687 (pdf)
Subjects: LCSH: Citizenship--Study and teaching--United States. | Digital media--Study and teaching--United States. | Media literacy--Study and teaching--United States. | Political participation--Technological innovations--United States. | Information society--United States.
Classification: LCC LC1091 .R727 2023 (print) | LCC LC1091 (ebook) | DDC 323.6071--dc23/eng/20221102
LC record available at https://lccn.loc.gov/2022050362
LC ebook record available at https://lccn.loc.gov/2022050363

Senior Acquisitions Editor and Developmental Editor: Valerie Witte
Copy Editor: Joanna Szabo
Proofreader: Linda Laflamme
Indexer: Valerie Haynes Perry
Book Design and Production: Danielle Foster
Cover Design: Christina DeYoung

First Edition

ISBN: 978-1-56484-966-3
Ebook version available

Printed in the United States of America

ISTE® is a registered trademark of the International Society for Technology in Education.

About ISTE

The International Society for Technology in Education (ISTE) is home to a passionate community of global educators who believe in the power of technology to transform teaching and learning, accelerate innovation and solve tough problems in education.

ISTE inspires the creation of solutions and connections that improve opportunities for all learners by delivering: practical guidance, evidence-based professional learning, virtual networks, thought-provoking events and the ISTE Standards. ISTE is also the leading publisher of books focused on technology in education. For more information or to become an ISTE member, visit iste.org. Subscribe to ISTE's YouTube channel and connect with ISTE on Twitter, Facebook and LinkedIn.

Related ISTE Titles

The Digital Citizenship Handbook for School Leaders: Fostering Positive Interactions Online by Mike Ribble and Marty Park (2019)

Digital Citizenship in Action: Empowering Students to Engage in Online Communities by Kristen Mattson (2017)

To see all books available from ISTE, please visit iste.org/books.

About the Authors

Carrie Rogers-Whitehead served as a youth services librarian for years, creating many programs and working with a broad range of patrons of all ages, abilities, ethnicities, social classes, etc. She left this position in 2016 and founded Digital Respons-Ability, the state provider of digital citizenship education in Utah. Carrie and her staff have trained tens of thousands of students, parents, and educators across the state and country on digital citizenship. Carrie is also an adjunct professor who regularly writes and speaks on technology, parenting, and digital citizenship. Her on-the-ground experiences have been shared in some of her other books, including *Digital Citizenship: Teaching Strategies and Practice from the Field* (2019) or *The 3 Ms of Fearless Digital Parenting: Proven Tools to Help You Raise Smart and Savvy Online Kids* (2021). Carrie lives in Utah with her family.

Vanessa Monterosa is an expert in digital literacy and education technology with more than 15 years of strategic planning and program development experience in the K–12 space. Her career and research focus has laid the groundwork for system-level digital citizenship implementation, most notably during her time as a district administrator in Los Angeles Unified where she developed key districtwide edtech policies and designed a digital citizenship program for leaders that served more than 14,000 educators. Vanessa has shared her experiences with many, writing for EdSurge, School Administrator, and Common Sense Media, and serving as the past co-chair of the ISTE Digital Citizenship Network. She has an Ed.M. in Technology, Innovation, and Education from Harvard Graduate School of Education and an Ed.D. in Educational Leadership from California State University, Long Beach.

Acknowledgments

Publisher's acknowledgments

ISTE gratefully acknowledges the contributions of the following:

ISTE Standards reviewers

McKenzie Fuller

Mia Gutsell

Lauren Mikulak

Julie Sessions

Manuscript reviewers

Darcy Calvillo

LeeAnn Lindsey

Amanda Nguyen

Kecia Ray

Analucia Tejada

> For Rick Gainsford, who was there for the beginning of the internet, and for the beginning of my digital citizenship journey. Thank you.
>
> —Carrie
>
> For Richard, Lilian, Denise, and Gary, who nurtured my love, interest, and passion for all things digital since childhood. And for Jordan who has cheered me on all along.
>
> —Vanessa

Contents

Introduction ix

PART I System-Level Considerations

Chapter 1 Digital Citizenship as a Change Initiative — 3
Case Study: A Story of Systemic Proportions — 4
Key #DigCit Levers for Change — 6
Organizational Leadership Frameworks — 9
Organizational Lens Approach: Policy Design — 16
Conceptualizing Digital Citizenship — 17
Chapter Wrap-Up — 18

Chapter 2 Creating Inclusive Districtwide Partnerships — 19
Case Study: Partnering to Build, Not to Fill — 20
Organizational Lens Approach: Partnerships — 23
Partnering with Internal Leaders — 25
Partnering with External Leaders — 28
Extending Partnership Opportunities — 30
Chapter Wrap-Up — 34

Chapter 3	**Professional Learning to Empower #DigCitLeaders**	**35**
	Case Study: Story of Cultivating #DigCitLeaders	36
	Organizational Lens Approach: Professional Learning	40
	Developing #DigCitLeaders	41
	Training for Change	47
	Chapter Wrap-Up	48

PART II Implementation and Practice

Chapter 4	**Examining Perceptions and Deepening Inclusivity**	**51**
	Avoiding a One-Size-Fits-All Approach	52
	Considering All Perspectives in the Conversation	53
	Case Study: Teaching Refugees	56
	Faith and Beliefs Around Digital Citizenship	57
	Finding a Shared Language	63
	Case Study: Teaching Youth in Custody	65
	Chapter Wrap-Up	66
Chapter 5	**Digital Citizenship for All Abilities**	**67**
	Teaching the Neurodivergent with Technology	68
	Neurodiversity and Communication	69
	Technology Use with People of Varying Abilities	71
	Case Study: Teaching Digital Citizenship at a State Hospital	77
	Case Study: Mental Illness and Technology Use	80

	What Can Educators Do?	82
	Chapter Wrap-Up	90
Chapter 6	**Learning from Community Partners and Policymakers**	**91**
	Navigating the Politics of Digital Citizenship	92
	Strategies for Managing Difficult Conversations	96
	Scaling Digital Citizenship	102
	Working with Elected Officials	107
	Chapter Wrap-Up	110
Chapter 7	**Implementing Digital Citizenship and the ISTE Standards**	**111**
	Classroom Tools for Moving Your Program Forward	112
	Strategies for Implementation	114
	Standards and Frameworks for Digital Citizenship Education	118
	Building a Culture of Ritual and Ceremony	122
	Teaching Digital Citizenship Across Grade Levels	123
	Planning for Digital Citizenship	127
	Chapter Wrap-Up	128
	Conclusion	**129**
	Appendix	**133**
	References	**142**
	Index	**148**

Introduction

A few years ago, I (Carrie) was starting the grueling process of scaling a digital citizenship program throughout my home state of Utah. I was having conversations and hiring people, and my staff and I were busy fielding questions and explaining not only our program but also what digital citizenship even meant. I was stressed. While I had project management experience, this was something different—it was changing a culture.

Around this time, I came across a dissertation by Dr. Vanessa M. Monterosa called "Digital Citizenship District-Wide: Examining the Organizational Evolution of an Initiative." I was excited. *She's done what I'm trying to do!* I messaged Vanessa and she graciously agreed to talk to me, an internet stranger, and share her research findings based on her experiences in Los Angeles Unified School District (LAUSD). Vanessa went on to different roles and work, and I continued to grow my program, but we kept in touch. Then the COVID-19 pandemic hit. Remote learning was quickly scaled (sometimes successfully, sometimes not so much) and it became even more clear that digital citizenship was needed. I reached out to Vanessa again. *So, how would you like to write a book with me?*

Here is that book, based on research, our previous publications (including that 2017 thesis), our experiences, and experts we rely on. It's also a book that comes from trial and error, having many, many conversations, and navigating politics and logistics. Change is hard. It's a winding road from policy to implementation. This book is designed to guide you toward cultivating key digital citizenship skills, mindsets, and dispositions from policy to practice.

This book is for the K–12 system-level leader—local, regional, and national—looking for clarity in how their high-impact role can support the implementation of a robust digital citizenship program. Digital citizenship has often been implemented by the few and the brave across our schools, but in order to provide students with a comprehensive, sustainable digital citizenship education, all leaders require an understanding of how we each contribute to this movement.

For the purposes of this book, digital citizenship is broadly defined as understanding the implications of our digital lives in the real world and harnessing this power for success and social good. We learned long ago that the most productive path toward developing digital citizens is to focus on what is possible and what is actionable to cultivate communities that empower and inspire both on and offline.

How the Book Is Organized

The book is divided into two parts, the first focusing on system-level considerations and the second focusing on digital citizenship work at the practitioner level.

Vanessa is the author of Part I, which addresses policy, partnerships, and professional learning at scale, and is grounded in theories of change. Part I will resonate most with system-level leaders, such as board members, superintendents, C-suite level leaders, district administrators, and general roles that have decision-making power. Part I guides the reader on system-level approaches to consider.

- Chapter 1 shares models and theories of building common ground with multiple stakeholders. Readers will learn about key types of policies to establish, such as a social media policy and acceptable use policy. The chapter also lays out frameworks for systemic change.

- Chapter 2 features case studies of partnerships around digital citizenship and how school and district leaders can bring the community together on this topic. Inter-departmental collaborations across different school roles are also discussed.

- In Chapter 3, the topic shifts to professional learning. From her experience guiding digital citizenship professional learning in LAUSD, Vanessa discusses how to create the structures and support for system-level implementation and how to align that learning with district policy. The ISTE Standards for Education Leaders will be covered as a framework for policy development in professional learning.

Halfway through the book, I take over with Part 2. When I'm talking to academics, I'm likely to describe myself as a "practitioner." That "figure-it-out-and-do-it" mindset of mine came about through years of working as a youth services librarian, when I had an opportunity to be in a space where I could serve people of all ages, abilities, ethnicities, classes, etc. I carried that mindset and experience working with everyone to founding my company, Digital Respons-Ability.

- With this perspective as a backdrop, Chapter 4 expands Vanessa's frameworks for systemic change into how we can make the practice of digital citizenship more inclusive. This chapter discusses disagreements, definitions, and perceptions of the school community around digital citizenship and technology in general. School leaders can benefit from descriptions of how to involve the whole community, and both leaders and educators will learn tips on how to actually make it happen.
- Chapter 5 goes into the teaching of digital citizenship for neurodiverse students. This chapter includes a case study with suggestions from practice and how technology can have different impacts on those whose brains work differently. Chapter 5 can help not only special ed teachers, but all teachers who have students with differing abilities and ways of thinking.
- Chapter 6 expands upon the conversation in Chapter 2 around finding common ground, discussing difficult conversations, marketing and outreach, and how to work with elected officials. School leaders can learn from the perspective of elected officials in this chapter. After reading Chapter 6, you'll have a better understanding of how to market, get feedback, and communicate more clearly about digital citizenship initiatives.
- The last chapter, Chapter 7, answers the question "How do we do it?" It shares how to use the ISTE Standards for Students across ages and abilities and gives advice on implementation of digital citizenship–related policy. Teachers across grade levels, but particularly elementary school, can get a better idea of how to teach digital citizenship from this last chapter.

Together, both parts of this book reflect the very kind of system-level approach digital citizenship needs: All levels of our school systems have to be involved. This book seeks to demonstrate how this is possible and why it is important.

Connections to the ISTE Standards

The book provides connections to the ISTE Standards as they relate to digital citizenship.

The **ISTE Standards for Education Leaders** support the implementation of the ISTE Standards for Students and the ISTE Standards for Educators, and provide a framework for guiding digital age learning. This section of the standards targets the knowledge and behaviors required for leaders to empower teachers and make student learning possible. They're focused on some of the most timely, yet enduring, topics in education today—equity, digital citizenship, visioneering, team and systems building, continuous improvement, and professional growth. This book synthesizes the ISTE Standards with organizational leadership frameworks to help system-level leaders address gaps in districtwide implementation. Each standard speaks to the importance of having a system-level mindset to move a digital citizenship program forward, especially one grounded in inclusion and equity.

EDUCATION LEADER STANDARDS

While education leaders are the focus of this book, we also address the following sections of the ISTE Standards where relevant:

- The **ISTE Standards for Educators** are designed to help teachers help students become empowered learners. These standards will deepen your practice, promote collaboration with peers, challenge you to rethink traditional approaches, and prepare students to drive their own learning.

- The **ISTE Standards for Students** emphasize the skills and qualities needed to engage and thrive in a connected, digital world. The standards are designed for use by educators across the curriculum, with every age student, with a goal of cultivating these skills throughout a student's academic career.

EDUCATOR STANDARDS

STUDENT STANDARDS

Additional Resources

In the Appendix, you can find example district policy templates, example board leadership documents, scope and sequence for implementation, and additional resources for system-level leaders.

Throughout the book, we've included QR codes linking to helpful resources to support your digital citizenship journey as an education leader.

Vanessa and I have created a website where we are putting links and lists to resources and research we consulted from this book. We also have downloadable documents to help you plan and evaluate your digital citizenship initiatives. This is a living website and more will be added. Check it out at deepeningdigitalcitizenship.org.

COMPANION SITE

Join Us!

We are both passionate about digital citizenship. We feel it's more necessary in the whole school community than ever. But we also know from our experiences that actually scaling, implementing, creating policies and structure, and teaching digital citizenship is not easy. We hope that this book can help others on their road from policy to practice. We both would have appreciated a book like this when we got started. We hope this will make your path less bumpy.

Let's travel this path together. Vanessa and I met on social media and learned from each other. We'd like to learn from your digital citizenship experiences, too.

Reach out to us there (@Digital_Empower and @DrMonterosa) and through our website deepeningdigitalcitizenship.org.

PART I

System-Level Considerations

In this section of the book, Vanessa shares approaches for building common ground with stakeholders, discussing key types of policies to establish, such as a social media policy and acceptable use policy. She also lays out frameworks for systemic change.

This section features a variety of case studies showing how school and district leaders can bring communities together and develop interdepartmental collaborations across different school roles. It also addresses professional learning, with an overview of how to create the structures and support for system-level implementation and how to align that learning with district policy.

Part I offers guidance on how to address gaps that may be present in your school system—for example, how to create empowering digital citizenship programs to better serve students if your school and district leaders do not agree on the meaning of digital citizenship. We encourage readers, no matter the size of their district, to consider the universal purpose of a policy: to reflect values in practice.

All chapters in Part I include an "Organizational Lens Approach" section to support you in leveraging key frameworks for your leadership practice.

CHAPTER 1

Digital Citizenship as a Change Initiative

There currently exists a plethora of resources to support teachers in classroom-level integration of digital citizenship, but supports and resources for system-level implementation remain limited. How can district and school leaders provide comprehensive support to implement key digital citizenship practices? This is the question I (Vanessa) set out to answer in 2014 working as a district administrator in the nation's second-largest school district, Los Angeles Unified (L.A. Unified).

This chapter speaks directly to system-level leaders within school districts—from principals of small schools or teachers leading departments to chief academic officers and division heads across districts. I'll provide an overview of organizational approaches and frameworks to examining digital citizenship on a system level, such as policy development, cross-departmental collaborations, and broad implementation. Moreover, this chapter demonstrates that digital citizenship implementation is more than just what happens in the classroom; leaders at all levels need to understand their roles in ensuring its effective implementation.

By the end of this chapter, you will:

- understand how to approach systemic change from an organizational leadership framework
- understand the important role of policy in shaping digital citizenship practices
- explore your organizational leadership paradigm with a lens toward digital citizenship implementation

Case Study: A Story of Systemic Proportions

I spent the early part of my career as a researcher studying the implications of social media for first-generation students, the opportunities afforded by game-based learning, and the impact of digital literacy. The more I engaged in these areas of scholarship, the more I realized that our practitioners needed immediate support and resources, so I left academia and landed in the nation's second largest school district—L.A. Unified.

> We knew we wanted to design a policy that not only included the necessary legalese but that also provided guidance on ways to be proactive, empowered digital citizens; a policy that spoke not only to students but to staff as well. More importantly, we wanted a policy that could be understood by those impacted by it.

At the time, L.A. Unified was in need of edtech policy expertise to support the district's one-to-one vision. In providing internet-ready devices to all students and staff, we knew that updated guidance around online learning and engagement was necessary. What set this district apart from others was that this call of innovative policy design originated from a board member. The board member acknowledged that current policies were preventing access to key digital resources because of outdated filtering rules grounded in fear-based perspectives. Additionally, they called for a social media policy for students and updated content for the employee version. In my first 10 weeks, I led our key district policy design and updates, infusing digital citizenship concepts into high-profile district policies. I ended up calling L.A. Unified my home for seven years as I was able to see our work flourish into a system-wide program, focusing on policy research, design, and development that was inclusive of the kind of digital-age learner and leader we wanted to cultivate.

To get started, we assembled a social media task force, which included voices from across the district from district senior leaders to school site staff. A critical voice that was missing, however, was that of the students. During our first meeting as a task force, we kicked off our session by collectively defining what social media means in regards to digital citizenship. Everyone noted down their best definition on a Post-it note and stuck it to the whiteboard. Responses ranged from "social media means online banking" to "social media is the internet," and digital citizenship was inextricably linked to cyberbullying. While both terms can be challenging to define, the polar differences in responses meant we needed to build a foundation of understanding together. How do we build consensus, I wondered, when we have varied perspectives?

During this time, I was engaged in my dissertation research (Monterosa, 2017), exploring what it meant to be a proactive, empowered digital citizen. My research was grounded in youth participatory practices in the digital age (Cohen & Kahne, 2012; Gleason & Von Gillern, 2018; Tynes & Monterosa, 2014; Soep, 2014), critical digital literacies (Kellner & Share, 2005; Jenkins, 2009), and the realities of youth growing up in an increasingly digital world (Boyd, 2014; Ito et al., 2009; Rafalow, 2020). This research informed my approach to policy design in L.A. Unified. As our team reviewed policies from comparable districts, we struggled to find an example that spoke to our aspirations for our district community. Instead, we found policies that were restrictive, limiting, and discipline focused—basically your run-of-the-mill acceptable use policy. We knew we wanted to design a policy that not only included the necessary legalese but that also provided guidance on ways to be proactive, empowered digital citizens; a policy that spoke not only to students but to staff as well. More importantly, we wanted a policy that could be understood by those impacted by it.

The first policy to be revised was our district's most high-profile and visible policy, requiring a signature by all students, legal guardians, and staff across the district: the Acceptable Use Policy (scan the QR code to view an example). This required a great deal of collective negotiating and bargaining across stakeholder groups—from staff to students. In creating a process to honor the voices of those the policy would impact, we ended up with a policy that was comprehensive, easy to understand, and aspirational. This policy experience served as the blueprint for future edtech policy updates, informing our subsequent Social Media Policy for Students and serving as a guide for our professional learning session design as well. The next section outlines steps you can take to design your own policy development process to support your system-wide digital citizenship implementation.

ACCEPTABLE USE POLICY EXAMPLE

In a system as large as L.A. Unified, policy served as the initial lever of change. Through my initial analysis, I noticed three key systems-level gaps:

- little consensus on conceptualization of digital citizenship
- lack of #DigCit-empowered educators leading the charge
- limited resources and supports for system-level implementation

In the rest of Part I, we'll examine these gaps and share strategies on how to address them to achieve system-wide implementation.

Key #DigCit Levers for Change

A plethora of resources are currently available to support teachers in classroom-level integration of digital citizenship, from Common Sense Education and elsewhere, but resources for system-level implementation remain limited (Monterosa, 2017). Moreover, these resources represent varied conceptualizations of digital citizenship, which result in inconsistent implementations of digital citizenship across classrooms, schools, and districts, which will be further covered in Chapter 4. While there is no single way to engage in digital citizenship implementation, it is important to establish a unified approach to what it means for your school and district community. One way to develop a unifying vision around digital citizenship is to consider its policy implications for your district (Ahn, Bivona, & DiScala, 2011; CoSN, 2013).

> While there is no single way to engage in digital citizenship implementation, it is important to establish a unified approach to what it means for your school and district community.

Designing a #DigCit Policy

Schools have a history of resisting technological innovations, with district policies often addressing digital initiatives with hesitation, such as limiting use and access to tools and websites and instituting policies that interfere with rather than facilitate the development of digital citizenship (Askari, Brandon, Galvin, & Greenhow, 2018; Culp, Honey, & Mandinach, 2005; Sánchez, Levin, & Del Riego, 2012). If you've written a policy for your school or district, you understand firsthand how challenging it can be to create a document that will speak to organizational and individual values and how we each show up in the world. For this reason, policies are often designed to outline the outcomes we don't want alongside the disciplinary actions that will take place if the policy is not adhered to. For example, the original acceptable use policy created for L.A. Unified focused on prohibited activities and actions, which is only part of what should be included in such a policy and does not provide the guidance required for successful implementation.

To design a policy that will support your digital citizenship program implementation, I recommend the following steps:

1. *Convene a cross section of stakeholders who will be impacted by the policy.* As illustrated in the experience shared at the beginning of this chapter, understandings of digital citizenship can differ widely. For this reason, it is critical to include not only the education leaders who will be responsible for implementing the policy but also representative students who will be impacted by it. Student voices are a critical component to policy design as further discussed in Chapter 2 and Chapter 6.

2. *Build consensus on definitions and conceptualizations around digital citizenship.* Digital citizenship is often equated with preventing cyberbullying, but our research at L.A. Unified pushed us beyond safety and privacy to include ways digital citizenship could be a proactive practice. In introducing this key research to our convened group, we were able to learn and immerse in these ideas together and develop a collective foundation of understanding. Merve Lapus, vice president of education outreach and engagement at Common Sense Media, encourages leaders to carefully consider policy design because "depending on the way you frame digital citizenship, the language and terms used can very easily become a very divisive thing. It is important to focus on dispositions rather than what is right or wrong." For instance, early on, our stakeholder community agreed that the term "acceptable" was not reflective of the kind of empowered digital citizen we wanted to cultivate. We wanted to cultivate responsible digital citizens. Thus, we amended the policy name to "Responsible Use Policy."

3. *Draft key policies related to digital citizenship.* Once we reached general consensus with our group, our team took everyone's best ideas and created a draft grounded in our shared language and understanding. This took several iterations, but taking the time to get it right at this stage proved to be helpful as we moved on in the policy design process. More importantly, our team was primed to be able to explain our initial decisions as we engaged in further dialog.

4. *Engage in participatory policy design.* In partnership with several schools across our district, we were able to put drafts of our policy in front of principals, teachers, and students across grade levels. We engaged them in close-read activities of the policies and incorporated their feedback such as clarifying concepts, writing in first person, and using language that is accessible to all. Through this participatory practice, what emerged loud and clear from our principals and teachers was the need to have the policy be structured as an instructional tool rather than merely a document to sign off (see Figure 1.1). This key feedback

and recommendation would not have emerged had we not taken time to listen to our practitioners on the ground. Thus, we designed a policy that could be used as an instructional resource in guiding students and staff in the responsible use of technology.

5. *Revisit and update your key policies annually.* Updating this policy resulted in strengthening the partnership among district educators and technical professionals as we worked collaboratively to iterate a version that would be easy to understand. See the Appendix for strategies and examples to create a version that resonates with your community.

Student Responsibility

By initialing and signing this policy, you acknowledge that you understand the following:

_____ I am responsible for practicing positive digital citizenship.
- ☐ I will practice positive digital citizenship, including appropriate behavior and contributions on websites, social media, discussion boards, media sharing sites, and all other electronic communications, including new technology.
- ☐ I will be honest in all digital communications.
- ☐ I understand that what I do and post online must not disrupt school activities or compromise school safety and security.

FIGURE 1.1 A policy that reflects stakeholder voice outlines the actions and behaviors you want to see from your community.

Cultivating #DigCit Cross-Collaborations

Policies reflect organizational values and traditions; they cannot be designed in a vacuum. Cross-collaboration is necessary for policies to reflect community values, especially because digital citizenship affects all aspects of the learning environment. In addition to the group you convene in the beginning, sustaining a successful digital citizenship implementation requires creating and maintaining ongoing collaborations.

Digital citizenship is often treated as a technical challenge before an instructional one, meaning that before you discuss it in the classroom, decisions about digital citizenship have already been made. With this in mind, do the following questions sound familiar?

- What websites should be blocked?
- Where should the routers at a school site be located for maximum connection?
- How strong should the filter be for online access?
- What do we need to look out for when it comes to cyberbullying on campus?

Digital citizenship requires the cross-collaboration of not only instructional leadership but also information technology (IT), mental health and counseling leaders, facilities leaders, and more. The specifics will depend largely on how your system is set up, but I encourage you to make a short list of key departments or teams who may need digital citizenship awareness (we'll dive into this more in Chapter 2). After drafting a policy and identifying potential collaborators, you are well on your way to creating system change.

So, you have your policy. You have identified cross-collaborators across domains. How do you put these levers to work in order to implement a comprehensive digital citizenship program? Change doesn't occur overnight. Let's look to system-level frameworks to help you take your program implementation to the next level.

Organizational Leadership Frameworks

Change at an organizational level is a systematic yet complex undertaking, especially when the change is centered on a concept and practice that is not fully realized, such as digital citizenship, and that requires significant capacity-building among students, families, and staff. When I was called to design and lead a system-level implementation of digital citizenship, there were no administrator-focused resources to guide me. So, as a scholar-practitioner, I used my research (Monterosa, 2017) to address this gap and leverage an organizational leadership framework to create a foundation for what a system-level digital citizenship implementation can look like in action. This book builds on this foundation by expanding what it means to implement digital citizenship from policy to practice. (Scan the QR code to learn more.)

DIGITAL CITIZENSHIP DISTRICT-WIDE

> Change at an organizational level is a systematic yet complex undertaking, especially when the change is centered on a concept and practice that is not fully realized, such as digital citizenship, and that requires significant capacity-building among students, families, and staff.

Following are three frameworks that will enable you as a school or district leader to understand the bird's-eye view while honoring the on-the-ground perspective (scan the QR codes to learn more):

- The Four-Frame Model (Bolman & Deal, 2013): An organizational leadership approach helps us unpack the complexities of a system-level change initiative.
- Prosci ADKAR Model for change management (Hiatt, 2006): A change management approach helps us understand our individual contributions in pushing forward a change initiative.
- ISTE Standards for Education Leaders (Crompton, 2018): This set of standards outlines skills and dispositions for being an empowered and inclusive education leader.

FOUR-FRAME MODEL

PROSCI ADKAR MODEL

ISTE STANDARDS FOR EDUCATION LEADERS

The Four-Frame Model

The Four-Frame Model (Bolman & Deal, 2013) provides an innovative lens through which to examine and critique a district's organizational approach to designing and implementing a digital citizenship initiative. Digital citizenship is often relegated to classroom-level discussion and engagement, despite the level of change and awareness necessary among education leaders to be productive, proactive digital citizen leaders, too. Using the Four-Frame Model provides a method of unpacking the complexities of an organizational change initiative, allowing the subtle nuances of cultivating a digital citizenship initiative to emerge.

The Four-Frame Model comprises four organizational frames: Structural, Human Resources, Symbolic, and Political, each of which highlights aspects that are critical to addressing organizational issues. Here is a breakdown of each frame:

Structural frame

- speaks to the importance of organization, systems, and maximizing resources and data
- relevant in identifying whether schools have the resources or systems in place to support and implement a digital citizenship curriculum
- requires that educators consider which key positions, procedures, and processes need to be in place to support digital citizenship education

Human Resources frame

- emphasizes the importance of people and relationships within the organization, which is fitting because a digital citizenship program necessitates leadership that understands its importance and the opportunities it can offer
- considers how a team as a whole works toward digital citizenship implementation that impacts both students and educators

Symbolic frame

- centers on vision, traditions, and interpretations
- enables stakeholders to consider how to develop and sustain their understanding of digital citizenship across a distributed leadership environment within a district, recognizing the need to cultivate a culture among students, teachers, and staff
- provides a lens to understand digital citizenship as a concept that extends beyond safety and security, facilitating stakeholder interpretations of what it means to be a digital citizen

Political frame

- focuses on mobilizing resources and building coalitions to effect change
- asserts that conflicts are ever-present in all relationships within and among organizations, facilitating decisions and processes along the way such as the conceptual tension of broadening digital citizenship beyond safety and privacy
- centers the role of policy in determining the trajectory of program design and implementation within a bureaucratic system, such as a large, urban school district
- fosters coalition building among stakeholders as a key thread in relation to digital citizenship

When frames are used together as a multi-frame tool, the complexities and nuances of change at an organizational level become salient, which discourse around digital citizenship implementation critically needs. Table 1.1 provides an overview of the key concepts for each frame.

TABLE 1.1 The Four-Frame Model

	STRUCTURAL	HUMAN RESOURCES	SYMBOLIC	POLITICAL
METAPHOR FOR ORGANIZATION	Factory or machine	Family	Carnival, temple, theater	Jungle
CENTRAL CONCEPTS	Roles, goals, policies, technology, environment	Needs, skills, relationships	Culture, meaning, metaphor, ritual, ceremony, stories, heroes	Power, conflict, competition, politics
IMAGE OF LEADERSHIP	Social architecture	Empowerment	Inspiration	Advocacy and political savvy
BASIC LEADERSHIP CHALLENGE	Attune structure to task, technology, environment	Align organizational and human needs	Create faith, meaning	Develop agenda and power base

Adapted from *Reframing Organizations* (Bolman & Deal, 2013, p. 19)

As mentioned, when used as a multi-frame tool, the Four-Frame Model provides a comprehensive understanding of organizational nuances that can help identify key points of change. So, how can you use this framework to inform your #DigCit policy development needs? Later in this chapter, we'll explore how to apply the Symbolic frame to guide your policy design effort. In Chapter 2 and Chapter 6, we will discuss partnerships through the lens of the Political frame. Chapter 3 and Chapter 7 will address the Human Resources and Structural frames.

ADKAR Change Management

Why do we need to change? What is the purpose? Why is this change needed at this time? Creating digital citizenship awareness at all levels of a district is founded on answering these questions. And managing change is not a one-time approach; it requires ongoing attention, care, and understanding, including working with stakeholders who may not be on board with the change and finding common ground to move forward. Moreover, designing a system-level approach to digital citizenship across a district requires an instructional paradigm shift that is gradual in its implementation and supported by a policy and human resource infrastructure that is prepared to address it.

With all this in mind, L.A. Unified leveraged the Prosci ADKAR Model for change management to support this shift toward district-wide digital citizenship practices for all learners.

> Designing a system-level approach to digital citizenship across a district requires an instructional paradigm shift that is gradual in its implementation and supported by a policy and human resource infrastructure that is prepared to address it.

The ADKAR Model (Hiatt, 2006) addresses the following goals for change:

- **A**wareness of the need to change
- **D**esire to participate and support the change
- **K**nowledge of how to change
- **A**bility to implement the change
- **R**einforcement to keep the change in place

For a very long time, digital citizenship meant cyber safety and security—keeping passwords safe, avoiding online stranger danger, etc. Because of this mindset, our IT leaders were initially hesitant to radically change how to discuss and approach addressing digital citizenship. My team's instructional vision of empowerment and influencing online civic engagement seemed at odds with IT perspectives. However, following the ADKAR Model, we were able to create awareness and desire to support the change and collectively work to unpack what we meant by empowerment. Our instructional team and our IT partners were then able to reconcile what seemed like differences but were really different points along a continuum of what it means to be an empowered digital citizen. Indeed, once you begin this journey, it is important to envision change management as a continuum—you will often revisit needs to create awareness while also addressing opportunities to reinforce the change by being able to meet stakeholders where they are.

A change management framework not only provides a roadmap on how to approach pushing change forward, but also reminds you to give grace where grace is due. Pushing a system through change is no easy task. It requires capacity-building at all levels to ensure the change effort has a strong foundation upon which to grow. In 2019, after hosting several Digital Citizenship Week (scan QR code to learn more) events aimed at learning experiences for students, our team hosted an event specifically for district administrators. It was the first our team had done, and it wasn't as flashy as our usual celebrations, but it was an opportunity to create awareness among all levels of district staff about digital citizenship, what it meant, and why it was important for them to know about it. The concept was simple: Set up a booth with digital citizenship resources in the common area of our district office with an interactive selfie station and a pledge poster to sign to demonstrate support. In doing so, our dedicated #DigCit team was able to build the capacity of leaders from our chief academic officer to charter school division leaders and facilities leaders. It was both a simple and effective way to plant the digital citizenship seed among various departments.

DIGITAL CITIZENSHIP WEEK

> Pushing a system through change is no easy task. It requires capacity-building at all levels to ensure the change effort has a strong foundation upon which to grow.

Digital citizenship is a challenging practice to define: Some associate it with anything that involves using a computer, whereas others solely focus on its relationship to cyberbullying. But by breaking down the path toward change with the ADKAR Model as a framework, it becomes easier to target the necessary areas where greater capacity-building is needed.

ISTE STANDARDS FOR EDUCATION LEADERS

The ISTE Standards for Education Leaders (ISTE, 2018) are a set of skills and dispositions that reflect what our increasingly digital learning environments need in terms of school and district leadership.

- *Equity and Citizenship Advocate:* Leaders use technology to increase equity, inclusion, and digital citizenship practices.
- *Visionary Planner:* Leaders engage others in establishing a vision, strategic plan and ongoing evaluation cycle for transforming learning with technology.
- *Empowering Leader:* Leaders create a culture where teachers and learners are empowered to use technology in innovative ways to enrich teaching and learning.
- *Systems Designer:* Leaders build teams and systems to implement, sustain and continually improve the use of technology to support learning.
- *Connected Learner:* Leaders model and promote continuous professional learning for themselves and others.

Each standard speaks to the importance of having a system-level mindset to move a digital citizenship program forward, especially one grounded in inclusion and equity. The Visionary Planner, Empowering Leader, and Systems Designer standards reflect what we have discussed in this chapter so far, from empowering digital citizenship practices to organizational leadership frameworks. Synthesizing instructional standards, such as the ISTE Standards, with organizational leadership frameworks further strengthens our ability to address gaps in your system and implementation. The Connected Learner standard will come into play when we discuss professional learning opportunities for leaders. In Part II, we will revisit some of these Standards as well as address the Equity and Citizenship Advocate standard as we share approaches on communication and inclusion of diverse perspectives from across the school community.

RELATED ISTE STANDARDS

Leveraging a change management framework to guide your system-level implementation and ensuring stakeholders have a say in policy design enables you to be a Visionary Planner. These strategies support you and your team in collectively creating a shared vision for digital citizenship.

ISTE STANDARDS FOR EDUCATION LEADERS: 3.2 VISIONARY PLANNER

- 3.2.a. Engage education stakeholders in developing and adopting a shared vision for using technology to improve student success, informed by the learning sciences.

Organizational Lens Approach: Policy Design

When it comes to policy design, the Symbolic frame in particular can be illuminating. From this frame, an organization is perceived as a culture comprised of compelling stories, strong values, and established traditions (Bolman & Deal, 2013). Bolman and Deal (2013) define culture as both a product and process, where the product is reflected in the wisdom and experience of the organization and the process is reflected in the organization's renewed and recreated traditions as more stakeholders come on board. Over time, districts often demonstrate a shift in their story, values, and traditions when implementing digital citizenship programs and policies.

According to the Symbolic frame, an organization's values characterize its position on an issue, impacting its traditions and overall narratives. Thus, as districts typically value safety and security above all else, these values dictate the way technology is addressed in the classroom and how it is discussed across policies. For example, in relation to values, there is overlap between the Political and Symbolic frames. The Symbolic frame thrives on values, because core values are what characterize an organization. For the Political frame, values play an important role in that differing values are negotiated to determine a more unified, comprehensive set of values that represent multiple stakeholders. Thus, as district values expand to embrace empowerment through digital means, the bureaucratic processes and procedures will soon follow, which can be observed through both the Symbolic and Political frames.

A shift in values allows for the development of policies that embrace an initiative focused on productive ways of engaging online. The L.A. Unified example of transforming an acceptable use policy into a responsible use policy illustrates this, in that the change reflected the growth and understanding from the collective group of stakeholders. Teachers and principals understood the importance of these policies and wanted these key documents to reflect their importance in the policy's design, making for an accessible policy for all stakeholders. Rather than a wall of legalese, teachers and principals wanted language and concepts they could work with and leverage as an instructional guide with students and families. However, our L.A. Unified legal department also wanted to ensure our district policies adhered to necessary federal laws. How did we strike a balance? By finding a common ground in designing a policy with the necessary legal component alongside accessible concepts and language that our educators could use to kickstart digital citizenship conversations with students and families: true participatory policy design at work!

From a change management perspective, policies help create awareness of how your district approaches digital citizenship. Updating a high-profile, highly visible policy further creates awareness among all stakeholders. If the policy were updated with stakeholder voice, it would underscore the desire to support the practices outlined in the policy. A change management perspective helps you keep a pulse on the steps necessary to build and sustain momentum in addition to clarity around implementation of an initiative. Lastly, approaching digital citizenship policy design from a Symbolic frame and ensuring appropriate measures to create awareness and engagement further illustrate what it means to be an Equity and Citizenship Advocate per the ISTE Standards. That is, first and foremost, you are ensuring that the safe, ethical, and legal use of technology can support the responsible and empowered digital citizen you hope to cultivate.

Conceptualizing Digital Citizenship

"Inclusive," "proactive," "empowered"—these are the terms I have used to describe our approach to digital citizenship in this chapter, and you will find these recurring themes throughout our book. As we share strategies and frameworks to inform your practice, it is important that we are also transparent about what we mean when we talk about digital citizenship. Digital citizenship, in its current and popular form, remains a concept that encompasses a wide range of topics, from identity to safety and from privacy to many forms of literacies. The perspective toward digital citizenship found in this book closely aligns digital citizenship with critical media literacies. Digital citizenship programs that look beyond safety and privacy concerns enable youth to discover how they can make a mark on today's world and engage in it productively rather than simply being told what not to do and how not to interact. Given that digital spaces are a prevalent method of communicating and engaging while it continues to shape all our lives in social and political ways, it is important to consider the relationship between digital citizenship and critical media literacy.

Critical media literacy is defined not only by deep analysis of media but also in assessing the sociopolitical ways media is constructed, empowering the consumer to understand both the stated and unstated intentions of a media artifact (Kellner & Share, 2005; Morrell, 2002). When it comes to participating in digital spaces, the barrier to entry into global conversations is lowered, because anyone with access to a device and the internet can create a digital account and engage with others. In creating their own media, today's youth exist in an increasingly participatory culture where digital spaces provide an outlet for them to exert both their voice and influence regarding social issues (Cohen & Kahne, 2012; Jenkins, 2009; Soep, 2014). Privacy concerns and the vulnerability of youth online are topics that occupy much of the literature on digital citizenship, but we want to expand this understanding. We want to add to the body of work in expanding digital citizenship from a fear-based practice to one about empowerment and real change.

Chapter Wrap-Up

In this chapter, we covered the importance of having an organizational approach to digital citizenship. To illustrate what it means to lead through change on a system level, I (Vanessa) shared the journey of L.A. Unified, where the district adopted the ISTE Standards and leveraged Common Sense Education resources, especially Digital Citizenship Certification opportunities and Digital Citizenship Week. Through these efforts, all involved were able to bring the ISTE Standards to life as Visionary Planners.

However, efforts on this scale require more than a vision—they require partnerships. Cultivating a digital citizenship culture in the nation's second-largest school district meant this work could not be done alone and was truly made possible by many key partnerships, which we will explore in Chapter 2.

CHAPTER 2

Creating Inclusive Districtwide Partnerships

What does it mean to provide system-level digital citizenship supports? As policies help shape a district's culture, it is important for system-level leaders to cultivate key partnerships to underscore their vision for digital citizenship. For instance, how often do IT leaders define digital citizenship as safety, privacy, and security while instructional leaders see digital citizenship as a practice inclusive of community, collaboration, and connection?

This chapter will discuss important interdepartmental as well as external collaborations and partnership opportunities to consider in creating a system-level approach to digital citizenship implementation. Readers will develop strategies to build coherence across different teams and departments to ensure deepened digital citizenship implementation.

By the end of this chapter, you will:

- learn how to determine your organizational approach to both internal and external partnerships
- get strategies for developing cross-collaborations to engage for digital citizenship implementation
- understand the kinds of partnerships to focus on to build digital citizenship capacity across your system and beyond

Case Study: Partnering to Build, Not to Fill

Partnerships can come in many shapes and sizes. Recently, especially at the start of the pandemic, potential partners in the digital citizenship space exploded. Many nonprofits and corporations began reaching out to school leaders, extending opportunities to support during a significant time of need. For example, *EdTech Magazine* and *Tech & Learning* invited the L.A. Unified district's team to present at corporate events and share how private industry might be able to support and identify promising practices. In such interactions, it was important to consider what the mutually beneficial exchange would be. Many system-level leaders had yet to establish external partnerships that supported online engagement and learning, let alone develop internal coherence, such as identifying and leveraging key organizational partners, strategies, and needs about their approach. As discussed in Chapter 1, digital citizenship requires intentional capacity-building and awareness efforts among education leaders systemwide. I (Vanessa) served as a district administrator during the early stages of the COVID-19 pandemic, and it was incredibly challenging and stressful. Thankfully, our L.A. Unified team had put some building blocks in place to support our transition to online learning, putting our digital citizenship efforts into overdrive. Times were still incredibly tough, but the fruits of our partnership labor sprouted in ways that benefited our school and district communities.

> An important component of our change management initiative was to influence the age at which students begin learning about digital citizenship, as it had primarily been seen as a topic for high school students. We expanded our efforts to ensure that schools across grade levels were able to demonstrate that the topic was also relevant and important for younger students.

In June 2016, L.A. Unified became the first district in the nation to adopt the refreshed ISTE Standards for Students, which was the start of a robust partnership to support digital citizenship education for all stakeholders. To support our digital citizenship implementation, our team leveraged our long-standing relationship with Common Sense Education, who served as a collaborative sponsor for our annual Digital Citizenship Week (DCW) ceremonies starting in 2014.

According to the Common Sense Education site, DCW was created "to highlight the importance of helping kids, families, and teachers navigate our 24/7 digital world" (Common Sense, 2022). The goal is to spotlight how digital citizenship impacts the lives of students and engage them in high-impact activities such as finding credible news sources, learning how to balance media usage, and developing strategies around managing a digital footprint.

How exactly you implement your goals is always evolving based on developments in the field, and the approaches the event has taken over time have changed as well. For example, in its early iterations, our DCWs were about fanfare and calling attention to the importance of digital citizenship practices. To that end, young Disney stars would headline our events, giving brief speeches to our students about the impact of their digital footprint as an adolescent. Common Sense Media supported us in developing curriculum, but they also served as thought partners while we expanded our implementation. As an early initiative, having celebrity power at events was a great way to get attention from all stakeholders. Scan the QR code to view a tweet that shows Disney stars posing with students during a Digital Citizenship Week event.

However, it was important to begin transitioning from flashy events to substantive events sharing strategies and elevating our school communities. As our initiative matured, DCW turned into an opportunity to spotlight the strides our educators and students were making in becoming empowered digital citizens. For example, a school was selected each year as an exemplary digital citizenship showcase school, where students and staff were able to share their digital citizenship growth and how it was impacting their learning. Early in our initiative, we mainly celebrated DCW at secondary schools, supporting and hosting student panels where participants talked about what digital citizenship meant to them. However, an important component of our change management initiative was to influence the age at which students begin learning about digital citizenship, as it had primarily been seen as a topic for high school students. We expanded our efforts to ensure that schools across grade levels were able to demonstrate that the topic was also relevant and important for younger students.

One year in particular, we celebrated DCW at an elementary school. What does a digital citizenship celebration look like for our youngest learners? In partnering with their school's drama teacher, we were able to design a digital citizenship performance where students acted out scenarios that called

TEENAGE CELEBRITIES AT DIGITAL CITIZENSHIP WEEK

for positive digital citizenship. Partnering with a school site leader helped bridge our system-level approach to digital citizenship with the local needs of the school community. At this particular school, they were early in their journey in building digital citizenship coherence across their classrooms. For this reason, the drama teacher shared that it would be beneficial to their school community if we covered more entry-level concepts of digital citizenship, such as safety and privacy. Safety, privacy, and security are foundational to getting the digital citizenship conversation started and moving toward practices of empowerment. So, we met with the drama teacher weekly via phone calls and/or in-person meetings to brainstorm, identify key concepts, and design vignettes that could bring to life in a theatrical way the kinds of behaviors and actions that reflect an empowered digital citizen. You can see the results by scanning the QR code to view the student-led performance that addressed etiquette on the internet.

STUDENT-LED PERFORMANCE ABOUT "NETIQUETTE"

> In the middle of a pandemic, we still managed to hold our annual DCW, this time livestreamed for our schools to join, and we were able to celebrate the tenacity of our burgeoning digital leaders. This work could not be done alone.

The evolution of our DCWs alone was a testament to a steady and consistent effort to grow a movement across 720 square miles. In the middle of a pandemic, we still managed to hold our annual DCW, this time livestreamed for our schools to join, and we were able to celebrate the tenacity of our burgeoning digital leaders. This work could not be done alone. It was great to have a national organization such as Common Sense Education as a partner in our early stages because their wide-reaching platform helped to inform our program development. Moreover, we knew that nowhere else in the nation was there a dedicated team in place pushing forth a systemwide digital citizenship initiative. This meant that we had a full team looking for partners who would help us build.

Traditionally, partnerships are leveraged to address a gap in resources or program development. Because we had already collectively shaped our vision and goals for digital citizenship as a school community, we sought to continue personalizing our implementation and partnered with organizations who were willing to build alongside us. It was important that our partnerships were nimble and collaborative. We did not partner with organizations to address a gap in our supports; instead, we co-designed supports with our district communities in mind. While this approach took more time, it helped us meet our school communities where they were in their digital citizenship journeys.

Organizational Lens Approach: Partnerships

With the Political frame, bargaining and negotiating are key, and nuances of relationships, power, and resources emerge, which are critical to implementing initiatives across large systems. The Political frame in Bolman and Deal's (2013) Four-Frame Model comprises five propositions that guide the application of the frame:

1. **Organizations comprise coalitions of various stakeholders, from individuals to interest groups.** District initiatives often involve not only the district team who is leading the initiative but also require interdepartmental teams who have a stake in helping administrators, teachers, students, and families better understand digital citizenship. This can also apply to external partnerships, such as with nonprofits and private industry companies.

2. **Coalition members have differences in values, beliefs, information, interests, and perceptions.** In the context of this book, a coalition member can range from district leadership to teachers, students, and partners in this work alongside you. (In Chapter 4, we will cover navigating different perceptions in detail.) In many instances, the greatest degree of divergence in beliefs and interests often exists between *instructional* district leaders and district leaders who oversee the *technical infrastructure* for schools. From this frame, the varying deep-seated values and perceptions surrounding digital citizenship emerge, which range from viewing it purely as a safety and security initiative to believing in its ability to empower and mobilize students.

3. **Making decisions involves allocating scarce resources.** For example, decisions might involve mobilizing stakeholders to develop policies and district plans or putting staff in place to push an initiative forward.

4. **Scarce resources and differences put conflict at the center, making power an important asset.** The Political frame situates power among several sources and not simply by one's position of authority. For this reason, mobilizing groups of stakeholders is key to introducing and implementing more comprehensive digital citizenship policies.

5. **Goals and decisions emerge from bargaining and negotiating among coalition members.** From the Political frame, the evolution of an initiative can be perceived as a series of bargaining and negotiating instances over time. For example, due to L.A. Unified's distributed leadership composition and its size, bargaining and negotiating are the crux by which many decisions are made. In relation to digital citizenship, however, this framing served as one of the key ways digital citizenship was able to grow as a movement throughout the district.

Through the Political frame, the school district is an arena where an agenda, a set of rules, and multiple stakeholders are all vying for what satisfies their beliefs and interests. Through this frame, the distribution of power and the points of contention are more readily observable, the resources required to make change happen become clearer, and alliances needed to be cultivated can be more pointedly explored. As an arena, the school district is a complex ecosystem of multiple stakeholders with deep-seated values and circumstances where competing issues can transform into shared agreements through coalition-building, bargaining, and negotiation.

> As an arena, the school district is a complex ecosystem of multiple stakeholders with deep-seated values and circumstances where competing issues can transform into shared agreements through coalition-building, bargaining, and negotiation.

In the early stages of our digital citizenship initiative, L.A. Unified's health division was gearing up to launch a campaign called "Now Matters Later," which focused on the dangers of sexting, especially with the rise of Snapchat. The initial goal of the campaign was to scare teenagers into not using Snapchat or any other social media space, especially one where pictures could be posted, shared, and distributed. Given this was in the realm of social media and making informed decisions via online spaces, this was a great opportunity to incorporate digital citizenship. As an instructional leader, I was not equipped to lead discussions on predatory behavior of online strangers or the implications of sexting as distributing child pornography. I completely trusted and relied on our health division leads to build our capacity around these topics. By meeting with our health division leads, we were able to identify connection points in our values and circumstances around cultivating digital citizens who were aware of the pitfalls and were prepared with information and strategies to make informed, responsible decisions. Rather than telling students

> ## RELATED ISTE STANDARDS
>
> When aligning internal and external partnerships to your initiative, you are implementing ISTE Standard 3.4, Systems Designer. Considering partnerships requires you to think about the resources you have available and how you might creatively leverage collaborators to bridge the gap in resources. Indicator 3.4.d invites us as leaders to understand the gaps in our services and supports to help us identify partnerships that are values-aligned and can enhance digital citizenship efforts. Additionally, it asks us to consider how partnerships support our visions for digital citizenship, achieve learning priorities, and improve operations overall.
>
> **ISTE STANDARDS FOR EDUCATION LEADERS: 3.4 SYSTEMS DESIGNER**
>
> - 3.4.d Establish partnerships that support the strategic vision, achieve learning priorities and improve operations.

what they shouldn't do, we asked ourselves, what if we at least provided guidance on what they might do instead if faced with an uncomfortable or unsafe online circumstance? This internal collaboration also yielded early resources around navigating relationships in an online world among teenagers and served as an opportunity for instructional and mental health teams to learn from one another, building upon what it means to be a productive, positive digital citizen.

Partnering with Internal Leaders

In the early days of the L.A. Unified digital citizenship initiative, we approached it from a fear-based perspective, focusing primarily on safety, privacy, and security. Yet we were looking to grow beyond this necessary perspective to one of empowerment. How could we shift from protective to proactive conversations around digital citizenship? What we sorely needed was system coherence—all of our system leaders needed to come together to form a consensus on our definition and approach to digital citizenship in order to move forward. With this in mind, the following are examples of strategies for building a cohesive digital citizenship plan for your system when operating from an instructional lens:

- **Working with information technology leads:** By partnering with your IT department, you can help them broaden their definition of digital citizenship. IT will often solely focus on safety, privacy, and security matters, which are of great importance. However, by providing your instructional lens, IT leads will be able to make asset, filtering, and device decisions with what is most needed to cultivate a proactive digital citizen. Instructional and IT leads can collaboratively discuss digital citizenship from an aspirational perspective rather than outright blocking websites and not encouraging learners to be responsible digital citizens.

- **Working with facility leads:** Your facilities team often is responsible for the physical architecture and layout of resources where students spend hours learning. For example, if digital citizenship is an instructional component across all content areas (across each classroom and not simply relegated to computer lab time), this means placement of routers is an important facilities consideration to support digital engagement across a campus. Facilities teams are often the last to know or rarely included, yet their partnership can turn your pedagogical goals into physical reality.

- **Working with counseling and mental health leads:** Engaging in these digital spaces also has critical implications for their social and emotional learning, helping students foster purposeful, healthy interactions online (Livingstone & Stoilova, 2021). For example, mental health professionals can provide key insight to how you might discuss cyberbullying from a community wellness perspective. Counseling teams can collaborate with instructional leads to discuss the implications of digital footprints for college and career success.

Creating opportunities for interdepartment collaboration and coherence empowers key players across the system to contribute to digital citizenship implementation. Merve Lapus, vice president of education outreach and engagement at Common Sense Media, underscores the need for system-level implementation, sharing, "How do you work with educators, so they feel they can see themselves teaching digital citizenship? Build up their confidence in using digital citizenship resources, so they can meaningfully build it into their instruction. And then how do you work with administration to ensure that they're not a hurdle in implementation for schools" (interview, July 2022)?

To develop effective interdepartmental collaboration that involves administrative leaders positioning themselves as partners in digital citizenship implementation, consider the following strategies:

- **Identify stakeholder leads who are decision makers—or have access to and influence on the decision makers—and are integral to systemwide digital citizenship implementation.** Leads who are identified will depend on your system, policy design, and resources. Configurations can include an IT lead, instructional lead, mental health lead, legal representative, and a board liaison. This way, key aspects of your system are aligned in how to approach and integrate digital citizenship concepts relative to their focus area. Table 2.1 outlines various leads and their potential areas of focus.

TABLE 2.1 Stakeholder Leads and Focus Areas

	IT LEAD	INSTRUCTIONAL LEAD	BOARD MEMBER	LEGAL REPRESENTATIVE
Which frame?	Human Resources frame	Symbolic frame	Political frame	Structural frame
What focus?	System behaviors and infrastructure needs	Curriculum design	Policy and funding decisions	Compliance

- **Determine quarterly goals to collectively reach, such as awareness building of a key policy or the redesign and alignment of digital citizenship curriculum.** This may require an initial pre-collaboration session to engage in bargaining and negotiating, such as discussing resources, values, interests, and available information.

- **Set a bimonthly meeting to discuss implementation.** At this type of meeting, the anchor points are the key policies driving instructional, operational, and technical decisions. Team representatives can engage in collective problem solving. For example, if a policy calls for cultivating responsible digital citizenship and a school is requesting access to blocked websites, a team meeting topic around web filtering and instructional needs can surface. If a school reports a cyberbullying incident, there's an opportunity for a team meeting topic around positive behavior intervention that includes digital citizenship curriculum, rather than focusing purely on disciplinary actions.

Partnering with External Leaders

If you are early in your digital citizenship implementation, I encourage you to internally build capacity by engaging in collective discussions about what digital citizenship means to your school community (as discussed in Chapter 1) before diving into external partnerships. Doing an early assessment of where your collective agreement around digital citizenship lands will help inform your approach to partnerships and address any gaps in implementation you might have. For example, as a system leader, are you interested in adopting the values and beliefs of partners and learning from your partner in this capacity? Or are you interested in approaching partnerships by collaborating (e.g., bargaining and negotiating) to ensure the approach is personalized and mutually beneficial? Partnerships are key to supporting system-level initiatives, especially in resource-strapped environments, and there is no wrong way to approach them.

Now, let's take a look at forging partnerships outside of your organization. External leaders range from local nonprofits that might be doing localized work that is relevant to your community to corporate sponsors who have a stake in digital citizenship work. Until a few years ago, prominent digital citizenship curriculum leaders were few and far between. Presently, not only have more nonprofits entered the picture, but corporations have also joined the movement to influence digital citizenship practices.

Partnering with other organizations can bring great benefits, as well as a different level of complexity.

If you are considering an external partner, consider the following questions:

- How will this partnership be mutually beneficial for both parties?
- What deliverables will be produced as a result of this partnership, if any?
- How does the purpose of the partnership support systemwide instructional goals?
- What if the external partner's approach does not align with yours?
- Do you acquiesce to their requests or do you determine this is not a partnership for you at this time?

Here are some examples of what external partnerships might look like and what factors to consider as you explore these opportunities to deepen/expand your digital citizenship program.

Partnering with a Nonprofit

One local nonprofit whose work related to our work at L.A. Unified was an organization formed after the founder's child was a victim of cyberbullying. Based on his child's experience, the founder created a nonprofit in his child's name to prevent more families being affected by cyberbullying. The nonprofit's curriculum focused heavily on safety, privacy, and security in addition to highlighting all the potential dangers that can affect children. As explained in Chapter 1, safety and privacy are foundational elements to digital citizenship, but system-level leaders also want to have an eye toward skills, dispositions, and practices beyond being safe and secure online. While this work was aligned to some components of our district work, the nonprofit's efforts were driven by addressing and quelling fears that exist around safety and security, whereas our internal efforts were focused on addressing fears from an empowerment and awareness paradigm. This kind of partnership is ideal at the beginning of a system-level digital citizenship implementation. Many of our schools were early in their digital citizenship journey, and partnerships such as these can fill these early gaps to support a broad range of schools who are taking their first steps into digital citizenship practices. Yet, it is always important to keep the broader empowerment paradigm in full focus as you continue cultivating partnerships and expanding your digital citizenship efforts.

> It is always important to keep the broader empowerment paradigm in full focus as you continue cultivating partnerships and expanding your digital citizenship efforts.

Partnering with a Corporation

Partnering with a corporation presents its own unique set of challenges, especially if it is a big tech company (Lickteig, 2004; Sanders, 2005). Unlike local nonprofits, once a corporation is ready to partner, they have already invested millions of dollars in their product and product rollout (i.e., implementation). At this stage, it is often challenging to negotiate changes in curriculum and implementation with a corporate partner. From a Political frame, when a school or district with finite resources is offered an opportunity for a corporate partnership, power dynamics arise, as scarce resources and substantial differences put conflict at the center. When a big tech company is involved, their concept of digital citizenship will be one that aligns with their product.

Partnering with corporations requires explicit inquiries and discussions, especially when contracts are involved. Corporate partnerships can take on many forms while opening doors for great digital citizenship impact, and the Political frame helps you recognize that bargaining and negotiating are always an available—and often necessary—strategy for system leaders.

Extending Partnership Opportunities

Your systemwide digital citizenship impact can reach your school or district, but it can have ripple effects beyond your system as well. This can be in the form of collaborating with external partners for digital citizenship–focused events and amplifying initiatives, engaging in thought leadership work across external partner spaces, or advancing scholar-practitioner research through university collaborations. The opportunities are endless, and identifying strategic partnerships can further underscore the empowering #DigCit culture you aim to cultivate.

Need help determining partners or breathing new life into partnerships for digital citizenship work? Consider these opportunities:

- building momentum through Digital Citizenship Week
- memorializing lessons learned through thought partnership
- evaluating system impact through research-practice-partnerships

Digital Citizenship Week

As discussed at the beginning of this chapter, the annual Digital Citizenship Week (DCW) has grown in popularity over the years as more and more schools across the nation participate. It is important to consider DCW as an integral part of building a culture of empowering digital citizenship practices, especially to support the policies you have designed and want to implement.

During the first year of a district's digital citizenship initiative, you can hold small celebrations such as assemblies, signaling the district's new commitment to expanding its values. Over time, these annual celebrations often grow in size and awareness in addition to other efforts brought on through an initiative's implementation. The DCW celebration is one ceremonial effort practiced each year that serves to socialize new district staff into district practices, stabilize the district's policy enforcement, reassure stakeholders they are keeping up with digital age needs, and convey to external stakeholders that the district is making an effort to be a leader in digital citizenship program and policy development.

DCW can also serve as a key moment to demonstrate stories of exemplary digital citizenship implementation, which function to establish and perpetuate the organization's traditions (Bolman & Deal, 2013). In addition to district policies, stories of implementation help bring policy mandates to life and demonstrate how policies can be more than bland mandates. Sharing can happen in many forms to amplify your system's own digital citizenship impact. For example, if you are an instructional leader, consider co-designing your DCW with other internal departments, such as your information technology team or your mental health services team. By partnering with departments across the aisle, your DCW can take on different shades and shapes in demonstrating the breadth and depth of your systemwide vision. Furthermore, this approach proves that digital citizenship is not a practice relegated to the classroom—it impacts all aspects of your organization.

Partnering with external collaborators can often add another dimension to your DCW events. For example, identifying corporate partners that align with your system policies and culture serves as a crucial touchpoint for how you engage and discuss digital citizenship. Corporate partners often have their own approach to what digital citizenship means and should look like, such as Facebook's "Get Digital" resource (scan the QR code to learn more), which focuses on what digital citizenship looks like when fully using the Facebook platform. By intentionally partnering with corporate companies that occupy the #DigCit ecosystem, instructional leaders can begin to help shape the broader conversation around digital citizenship. Moreover, your school or district's initiative can be amplified and recognized in a multitude of ways, especially thought partnership and leadership opportunities.

GET DIGITAL

Thought Leadership and Partnership

Thought leadership and partnership on a topic of growing importance like digital citizenship is sorely needed. "Thought leadership" is when you memorialize your learning across various media—blogs, videos, publications, and more. "Thought partnership" is when you partner with others purely to discuss strategy, implementation, shared practices, and lessons learned, and offers spaces to simply support one another.

My first foray into thought leadership on behalf of the L.A. Unified team was a 2015 article in the Association for California School Administrator's (ACSA) magazine where I shared our early thinking on what digital citizenship might look like as we were working toward a system-level approach. Because I was looking to fill the resource-gap for administrators, it was important to share our latest thinking in spaces that had a large administrator readership. I ended my article with the following hope: "Through our Digital Citizenship Week, it is our hope to provide rich, timely information . . . [to] support teachers in implement[ing] digital citizenship education and gain[ing] momentum in continuing this important conversation moving forward" (Monterosa, 2015). Year after year, I committed to building out our digital citizenship supports, and along the way, I ensured our learnings were shared both internally and externally.

> External thought leadership not only lends credence to your initiative, but makes your efforts highly visible, increasing opportunities for grants, funding, partnerships, and more.

Memorializing your ongoing digital citizenship efforts is a key way to provide a foundation from which to learn and grow, especially in creating awareness and desire from a change-management perspective. Additionally, in outwardly sharing your system-level learnings, the opportunities to inform practice beyond your school or district walls increase. You might be wondering: Why would I want to make an impact beyond the community I am responsible for as a system leader? External thought leadership not only lends credence to your initiative, but makes your efforts highly visible, increasing opportunities for grants, funding, partnerships, and more. Fast forward to the end of my tenure at L.A. Unified, I co-presented a keynote at Facebook headquarters about the strides the nation's second largest district had made in expanding digital citizenship districtwide. An opportunity such as this would not have been possible had our team not intentionally shared our lessons learned to impact the field at large.

When establishing a partnership, inquiring about opportunities for publicizing, documenting, and memorializing your partnership is a great way to continue shaping values, beliefs, and information around digital citizenship. L.A. Unified's partnership with Common Sense Media created an opportunity to share lessons learned on a national platform. From short videos to blog posts, our team was provided with space to share stories from the field more broadly. As we began noticing the impact of thought leadership opportunities, this became a staple across our partnerships.

The following thought leadership and partnership opportunities are a few examples to consider:

- co-authoring a blog post on a partner website
- co-presenting at conferences or in webinars
- discussing a spotlight story authored by a third party
- cultivating a relationship with neighboring district leaders to share digital citizenship approaches

Topics can range from how you approached partnership in defining digital citizenship to how a product or program approach is supporting digital citizenship implementation.

Research-Practice Partnerships

Measuring digital citizenship remains a challenge (Choi, 2016; Choi, Glassman, & Cristol, 2017; Literat, 2014). Metrics have ranged from measuring clicks to determining how students approach a digital dilemma. In all aspects of evaluation, it is important to find opportunities to gather data on your digital citizenship implementation. Establishing research-practice partnerships (RPPs) is one strategy to both influence the field and invite opportunities for preliminary evaluations (Coburn & Penuel, 2016; Penuel & Gallagher, 2017).

Designing and sustaining an RPP requires cultivating relationships with local higher education institutions, especially with departments that teach graduate students. RPPs offer an opportunity to hear the latest research on burgeoning efforts like digital citizenship and allow practitioners to be in direct conversation with researchers. RPPs create a vibrant, two-way street for feedback and impact, especially in terms of helping to shape research agendas that can yield practitioner results. For example, the Connected Learning Lab from UC Irvine has partnered with local schools to determine how Minecraft intersects with digital citizenship (Tekinbas, Jagannath, Lyngs, & Slovák, 2021). (Scan the QR code to learn more.) Findings suggest that games like Minecraft create digital opportunities for students to practice key digital citizenship behaviors, such as being responsible online, collaborating safely, and serving as an upstander in times of need for others.

MINECRAFT EDUCATION EDITION

Institutions with graduate programs also create a pool of potential program evaluators who are eager to apply their skills in real time. Studying digital citizenship can take on many forms—from a sociological perspective to a pedagogical one. Whichever the paradigm, having an RPP in place can support initial evaluation needs as you look toward expanding a digital citizenship initiative.

Chapter Wrap-Up

In this chapter, we explored how establishing key internal and external partnerships and extending the impact of your digital citizenship initiative are critical, especially as digital citizenships remains a growing topic of importance. Moving an initiative toward system-level implementation most certainly requires all system leaders to work collaboratively, but the true change comes when those on the ground support efforts as well. From a change-management perspective, getting system leaders on board creates much-needed awareness, but how do you move from creating awareness to building desire to cultivate empowered digital citizens? The answer rests in building the capacity of your school leaders to serve as the digital citizenship role models your school community needs, which we will discuss in Chapter 3.

CHAPTER 3

Professional Learning to Empower #DigCitLeaders

What does professional learning in alignment with policy focused on digital citizenship look like for district leaders? Furthermore, what does professional learning grounded in the ISTE Standards for Education Leaders entail? Using the ISTE Standards as inspiration for policy development and for professional learning is key to cultivating leaders who are committed to digital citizenship, reflect the #DigCitCommit concepts, and demonstrate leadership from policy to practice.

In this chapter, readers will learn strategies to design, develop, and deliver professional learning that builds the capacity of district leaders to support a systemwide digital citizenship program implementation. Professional learning examples will demonstrate policy-to-practice alignment and will cover asynchronous learning opportunities as well.

By the end of this chapter, you will:

- design a professional learning experience inspired by the ISTE Standards
- examine an introductory professional learning session for school leaders on establishing a digital footprint
- understand how a change management approach can inform professional learning design

Case Study: Story of Cultivating #DigCitLeaders

In the first three years of our quest to expand digital citizenship districtwide across L.A. Unified, we had developed a basic awareness around key district policy updates, created a foundation of internal capacity-building efforts among district leaders, and established partnerships that were helping to move our initiative forward. Based on my (Vanessa's) research, we had ticked all the boxes of an organizational initiative—or so we thought. After further consideration, we began to realize that a key aspect of our programming was missing and was not available to any of our partners: professional learning on digital citizenship implementation for our school leaders.

There exists an abundance of digital citizenship curriculum resources for teachers to use in classrooms, but resources to support school leaders remain limited, and until recently, resources for district-level administrators appeared to be absent from the conversation altogether. (One more recent resource is *The Digital Citizenship Handbook for School Leaders* [Ribble & Park, 2019].) At the time, we were leveraging Common Sense Education resources, especially the Digital Citizenship Certification opportunities (now the Common Sense Recognition Program)—but even those were still largely aimed at educators in the classroom. As a district administrator, I wondered how we could codify our learnings and practices in ways to support our school leaders districtwide. Simply reviewing what teachers would do in the classroom wasn't enough. Differentiated supports to enable a true systemwide digital citizenship program were needed to flourish. If a teacher's role was to engage students in digital citizenship activities, what was the principal's role in supporting that teacher? In turn, what was a district administrator's role in ensuring a school principal could extend supports and resources to their staff? Thus began our team's efforts to design differentiated professional learning opportunities to address all aspects of digital citizenship system-level implementation. (Scan the QR codes to learn more about the resources mentioned here.)

DIGITAL CITIZENSHIP HANDBOOK FOR SCHOOL LEADERS

COMMON SENSE RECOGNITION PROGRAM

A key component of our professional learning sessions was ensuring exposure and understanding of district policies that supported digital citizenship instruction in the classroom. Both my research and my interactions with school leaders confirmed that many leaders understood the importance of digital citizenship for students but were not sure how relevant this content was for them as leaders. Digital citizenship was perceived as a classroom activity to be managed by teachers rather than a system-level initiative requiring resources to be mobilized, policies to develop, and collective capacity-building for everyone involved. Moreover, countless education leaders expressed hesitation around digital engagement themselves, stating they were scared to say the wrong thing or get fired for posting inappropriate content. Based on the awareness stage of the ADKAR Model for change management (Hiatt, 2006), I developed the Digital Presence Framework to help education leaders consider what social media engagement means for them (I'll discuss the framework in more detail later in the chapter), and I designed and piloted a two-hour professional learning module called "Digital Presence with Purpose" aimed at school principals and district leaders to demonstrate why digital citizenship has implications for them as well.

> As a district administrator, I wondered how we could codify our learnings and practices in ways to support our school leaders districtwide. Simply reviewing what teachers would do in the classroom wasn't enough.

The purpose of this initial session, grounded in the Digital Presence Framework, was to create a general awareness and desire around digital citizenship by demonstrating the importance of their digital footprint as school leaders and how they can serve as #DigCitLeaders. At the conclusion of the session, attendees were invited to plant a stake in the virtual ground and author their first post using the #DigCitLeaders hashtag; these are still visible today across Twitter, Facebook, and even LinkedIn. (Scan the QR code to view on Twitter.)

#DIGCITLEADERS TWITTER POSTS

I originally piloted this framework in August 2018 through a training with 27 instructional coaches who had varying levels of digital engagement interest. At the end of the 2018–2019 school year, nearly all pilot participants had established a "Digital Presence with Purpose," and continued to leverage their digital footprint to connect with their school community, amplify their contributions to their content areas, and collectively demonstrate their pedagogical expertise.

When the COVID-19 pandemic hit, those who had gone through this training were uniquely positioned to leverage social media in ways that kept them connected to their students, families, and staff. This is a trend we saw nationwide as educators took to social media to maintain a sense of community (Greenhow, Staudt Willet, & Galvin, 2021). Those who hadn't had the opportunity to engage prior to our emergency remote circumstances were able to join one of two professional learning webinars where I trained 14,000 educators in one week in April 2020. It was a pivotal realization that this introductory digital citizenship session for leaders was able to play a significant role in a time of crisis. Thus, this professional learning opportunity reflected the need to have a team in place not only to deliver the content, but also to personalize it to school leaders in ways other trainings had yet to engage them with digital citizenship content.

Digital Presence Framework

The Digital Presence Framework comprises the following three elements, which together will help education leaders build understanding around digital citizenship and the importance of their digital footprint to begin the journey toward becoming digital citizenship leaders (Monterosa, 2021).

- **Sharing Knowledge:** This sphere invites educators to contribute their learnings at a training session or conference event into meaningful, relevant examples that could be beneficial to other educators. For example, many of us have recently been attending countless webinars to understand how to navigate our remote learning circumstances. Have you gained valuable insight into how you will approach remote teaching and learning this fall? If so, this is an opportunity to share your knowledge and how you plan to implement key strategies to support students.

- **Sharing Resources:** This sphere invites educators to connect with others in sharing artifacts, research, or other sources informing their thinking and their practice. More importantly, your digital footprint begins demonstrating your growth mindset toward your identity as an education leader. Sharing resources that add value to your instructional or leadership practices demonstrates your commitment to your craft and can inspire others to do the same.

- **Sharing Evidence:** This sphere invites educators to uplift their school community by showcasing the rigorous, relevant instructional leadership activities they support through media-rich content. Consider sharing in-person and remote examples, such as video of schoolwide events, pictures of culminating student projects, certificates of trainings you completed, screencasts of students presenting their learnings, screenshots of Zoom meetings with colleagues as you plan to work through remote teaching, or a link to a webinar you led about a topic that resonates with your leadership approach.

For school leaders, the Digital Presence Framework ultimately provides a leadership lens in considering work, insights, and professional interests as source material for digital engagement and contributions. By engaging in this experience, school leaders get firsthand experience of the decisions students should consider as they lead an overwhelmingly digital life. When students step into the classroom, they often forfeit their digital engagement because school leaders are not embracing the opportunities afforded by these digital age practices and tools. Educators who remain hesitant to embrace the unfamiliar continue to stifle the essential awareness students need to consider how digital spaces can empower them. Thus, education leaders should be supported in designing professional learning experiences that involve participation in digital citizenship practices and challenging assumptions.

As our nation's school leaders work toward bridging the digital divide, the participatory divide waits to be addressed as well. More importantly, if your district includes both leaders and students of color, digital engagement and representation is even more important. In addition to contributing your voice and cultivating community and connection, you also ensure greater representation and increased visibility of all our efforts as educators. Our youth need role models that are savvy when it comes to participating in our digital economy and thus more accessible to them in their digital spaces, and this starts by establishing a digital presence with purpose as a digital age education leader.

> Educators who remain hesitant to embrace the unfamiliar continue to stifle the essential awareness students need to consider how digital spaces can empower them. Thus, education leaders should be supported in designing professional learning experiences that involve participation in digital citizenship practices and challenging assumptions.

Organizational Lens Approach: Professional Learning

The Structural and Human Resources frames of the Four-Frame Model (see Chapter 1 for an overview of the model) is often challenging to disentangle. Both speak to teams and the importance of capacity to push an initiative forward. However, the nuance appears when we consider training and the capacity of those trained to have processes and pathways to build the capacity of others. In other words, the Structural frame can be visualized by an organizational chart with its design hierarchy informed by the organization's overall goals and environment. The Human Resources frame illuminates how we invest in others and how they, in turn, serve still others (Bolman & Deal, 2013).

The Structural frame invites you to consider the resources available to carry out your organizational vision and ask the following questions:

- How has coordination among departments been mapped out to bring my district's digital citizenship initiative to life?
- What structural deficits need remedying and attention in my district's next digital citizenship program iteration?
- How have responsibilities been allocated, especially if the desired outcome is a digital citizenship implementation that focused on empowerment?

When thinking about professional learning, it is important to differentiate learning experiences for leaders, and considering where they fall from a structural perspective can help you decide who needs what training at the appropriate time.

The Human Resources frame highlights how the skills, attitudes, energy, and commitment of staff are critical to sustaining organizational initiatives. For a systemwide digital citizenship initiative, it takes more than just curriculum in the classroom. It requires an all-hands-on-deck approach—from our teachers to principals and from district administrators to board members. For this reason, the Human Resources frame allows you to consider opportunities to build the capacity of leaders across your system in personalized ways, centering how you make an initiative a meaningful endeavor for all involved. Put simply, the Human Resources frame forces us all to consider "What's in it for me? What's in it for you?" For example, why should a leader on the facilities team care about digital citizenship? What does capacity-building look like for law enforcement when it comes to empowering digital citizenship concepts and practices? A systemwide initiative requires the time and resource investment to develop a cadre of committed leaders.

If you are about to embark on designing a systemwide digital citizenship program from policy to practice, focusing on the strategy and what your school leaders need (using the Structural and Human Resources frames) can help you take the first steps to consider what it can look like behind policy development. In addition to the Four-Frame Model, leveraging an ADKAR Model as a change management lens further underscores the need to create awareness, build stakeholder desire to be a part of the change, and create opportunities to learn how to be a part of the change. In addressing this early part of change management, you can then focus on expanding opportunities to train others, ultimately reaching the point of reinforcing ideas and practices throughout the system (Hiatt, 2006).

For the purposes of this chapter, we'll assume that you have engaged in collective conceptualization of digital citizenship with a variety of stakeholders, which we'll discuss more specifically in Chapter 6. You've then developed an aspirational policy that reflects community needs and agreements around digital citizenship. You've identified key internal and external partnerships to build and sustain momentum of your initiative. But partnerships can take you only so far without the support and championing of your most essential stakeholder group: school leaders. This chapter focuses on how professional learning is an integral component to a systemwide digital citizenship initiative, where you model how to be an empowering leader per the ISTE Standards. As an empowering leader, you empower educators to exercise professional agency and create opportunities for personalized professional learning. Furthermore, an empowered leader helps build the confidence and competency of their staff across their organization.

Developing #DigCitLeaders

When it comes to digital citizenship, the first stakeholders that come to mind are often students. What immediately follows are initial fear-based thoughts relative to digital citizenship—horror stories of young adults posting content without considering the ramifications of their decisions, cyberbullying incidents, students losing jobs and college offers, etc. (Boyd, 2008; Singer, 2013). After seeing how real-life consequences result from actions in the digital space, it's no wonder there has been a plethora of resources designed to support teachers in building the digital literacy capacity of students. During my tenure in L.A. Unified, I witnessed many reports of cyberbullying incidents and school leaders asking for guidance on how to mitigate these occurrences. Was the answer to limit access to the internet? Collect mobile phones at the start of classes? Impose strict disciplinary action should these behaviors continue? Set up stricter firewall security to prevent specific website access? As a team, we grappled with these questions and more alongside our school leaders.

However, through research I came to understand that these questions positioned the tool as the problem rather than addressing the behavior in conjunction with the affordances of digital spaces. The more I debriefed with our school leaders, the more I realized they were not present in the digital spaces that our students occupied. During one of my modules, a participant shared, "I've always kept my social media profiles separate because I never wanted to get in trouble for anything I'd post or want my students to follow me. But now that I think about it, I understand how being visible as a school leader can help me role model what it means to be a good digital citizen." Thus, their solutions were driven by a limited understanding of online engagement dynamics, and when I pressed our educators to share more, they admitted a fear of saying the wrong thing, reflecting poorly on their school community—or worse, getting fired (Monterosa, 2021).

Across our nation's schools, I've found very few system-level examples of district leaders incorporating robust digital citizenship programs into educator guidelines or training. For example, talking about social media as an instructional opportunity remains a gray area for countless education leaders. Yet, we all know our students are already in those spaces, so how can we best support them if we aren't in those spaces as well? As resources continue to be developed to support students, where are the resources for the education leader?

Since system-level digital citizenship resources remains a burgeoning content area, I designed an educator-focused professional learning module that positions social media as a critical space for professional growth and engagement, essentially demonstrating what it means to be a connected learner per the ISTE Standards for Education Leaders: "using technology to regularly engage in reflective practices that support personal and professional growth" (indicator 3.5.c) while developing the skills needed to lead and navigate change. Up until I left L.A. Unified, I led every "Digital Presence with Purpose" module, iterating each time based on feedback from our system-level leaders. I usually delivered it during after-school hours to support school leaders in being able to join and engage in the session. Much of the session was dedicated to helping school leaders grapple with what digital citizenship means for them as highly-visible leaders in the community—not what digital citizenship means for students. For instance, after the first session, participants requested additional time to put their newfound knowledge into action. This meant refining the hands-on, interactive portion and ensuring sufficient time to support participants in applying their learning. Overall, I learned that very few educators had actively considered what digital citizenship might mean for them as leaders, so creating enough time and space to process this knowledge was key.

> Talking about social media as an instructional opportunity remains a gray area for countless education leaders. Yet, we all know our students are already in those spaces, so how can we best support them if we aren't in those spaces as well?

The professional learning module was truly about building school leaders' capacity to put themselves in the shoes of students making decisions on how to engage and interact online, grappling with the implications of what they share and how they share it. However, this session was not meant to demonstrate the dark side of online engagement, which I believed we all knew too well; it was meant to highlight the possibilities of online engagement to help school leaders envision the affordances of digital citizenship when focused on empowerment and civic engagement. For example, we talked about cultivating a digital footprint that could augment their own careers as school leaders wanting to advance in the district. As a system-level leader, if this was your goal, consider the following questions:

- How would an empowering orientation toward your own digital footprint influence your engagement and participation in connecting with others?
- How would that shape the pictures and content you would share?
- How would that impact the digital spaces you occupy and engage in?
- How would that inform those you follow and those who follow you back?

Shifting their mindset toward these possibilities helped school leaders uncover why their role in supporting a robust digital citizenship was critical and motivated them to ask questions about how they could further support their teachers in building out empowering digital citizenship communities at their school.

Having a digital presence with purpose is critical to your development as digital age education leaders. Some may consider this an exercise in personal branding. However, branding often connotes competition, differentiation, and establishing a loyal base. Reframing from branding to "digital presence with purpose" is to focus on contribution, community, and connection. A digital presence with purpose is more than having a static online profile with a few basic details about you as a professional; it requires being engaged, visible, and authentic. Essentially, this professional learning experience demonstrated what district policy in practice looks like for leaders, so they could develop insight into how this plays out for their staff and students. The session invited school leaders to model the very behaviors we all want to see in our empowered digital citizens across our classrooms.

RELATED ISTE STANDARDS

Digital citizenship is often thought of as a student-focused domain—something that students need to learn about. However, digital citizenship is each of our responsibility, and the ISTE Standards for Education Leaders help highlight the necessary skills and dispositions that we as education leaders must embody and model. For instance, an education leader who curates a digital presence with purpose is one who can engage as a Visionary Planner. Empowering education leaders to practice digital citizenship in very real ways, such as through social media, enables them to share their learning and influence their communities in real time. Additionally, it enables education leaders to serve as Connected Learners who engage in continuous professional learning as they design and deliver digital citizenship training to lead and drive change in their community.

ISTE STANDARDS FOR EDUCATION LEADERS: 3.2 VISIONARY PLANNER

- 3.2.e Share lessons learned, best practices, challenges and the impact of learning with technology with other education leaders who want to learn from this work.

ISTE STANDARDS FOR EDUCATION LEADERS: 3.5 CONNECTED LEARNERS

- 3.5.b Participate regularly in online professional learning networks to collaboratively learn with and mentor other professionals.
- 3.5.d Develop the skills needed to lead and navigate change, advance systems and promote a mindset of continuous improvement for how technology can improve learning.

Designing an Interactive Session for #DigCitLeaders

When adult learners are given a structured opportunity to experience digital engagement in productive and constructive ways, they become producers rather than consumers of content and are able to develop an understanding of their digital participation in relation to their participation in society (Jenkins, 2009). Thus, to invite educators to explore what digital citizenship means for them, as mentioned earlier in the chapter, I designed a module grounded in the Digital Presence Framework called "Digital Presence with Purpose," which focuses on practices of contribution through sharing knowledge, sharing evidence, and sharing resources responsibly. The session comprised the following:

- A **digital dilemma inclusion activity** for leaders with questions that elicited creative tensions encouraging deep dialog (James, Weinstein, & Mendoza, 2019). For example, with little context, I would invite participants to stand up and migrate to the side of the room according to the arrows on the slide and their responses to the prompt. One prompt read: *It is better that your digital footprint . . . be an authentic representation of who you are* OR *be an actively curated representation of who you are.* The activity created lively debate, especially as all my school leader participants would respond in terms of what they thought was best for students. When I pressed them to respond to this for themselves, the answers would often shift. There was no right answer, but it invited participants to begin thinking about digital citizenship as a practice for them as well and not solely for students.

- A **digital citizenship definition discussion** where leaders described what it meant to them based on their inclusion activity engagement (Monterosa, 2021). The definition I devised for L.A. Unified was based on scholarship around online engagement and empowerment: "The practice of cultivating a positive, authentic digital footprint that can be leveraged for college and career success." This definition may not work across the board, but it was an anchor point that reflected our values, beliefs, and aspirational outcome for a productive, positive digital citizenship program.

- A **district policy discussion** where leaders engaged in a jigsaw activity, examining three key policies meant to influence digital citizenship instruction and implementation. Reading policy is rarely fun, but including this portion as part of a professional learning session ensured increased awareness of key policies that could support the aspirational practices we were engaging in; thus, it supported practitioners in feeling less fearful to support innovative digital citizenship practices. In many cases, the professional learning session was the first time school leaders became aware that L.A. Unified had a social media policy in place for both students and employees.

- A **digital footprint analysis activity** where leaders learned how to conduct a targeted search engine inquiry to examine their own digital footprint and how that might reflect on their identity as a school leader. For this portion of the session, school leaders essentially spent time googling their own digital footprint. During this portion of the training, I would hear audible gasps as leaders discovered more of their personal information online than they had realized.

- A **debrief of their digital footprint analysis** where leaders engaged in identifying the Strengths, Weaknesses, Opportunities, and Threats of their digital footprint findings (SWOT). For many of my participants, it was the first time they realized they had an active digital footprint that they had never authorized to be created in the first place. For instance, during the L.A. Unified teacher strike of 2018, many educators found themselves across Google images and news articles. Others were reminded of accounts they had started long ago but hadn't kept up. As I invited participants to consider how their digital footprint might support their career, they began to note what steps they might take differently to demonstrate intentionality as a digital citizen. For example, if there was an aspect of their digital footprint that had yet to reflect their values as an education leader, they could actively consider what content to share according to the Digital Presence Framework that could further develop their footprint.

- A **review of the Digital Presence Framework** where leaders considered the powerful example they could set by becoming digital citizenship role models for their school community. This portion of the training was meant to build upon the SWOT they conducted in reviewing what already existed of their digital footprint. Additionally, this framework was meant to empower them to actively engage as a digital citizen and experience first-hand the private action of posting that results in public displays of engagement.

- A **hands-on, interactive portion** where I invited leaders to create or update a digital profile of their choice, such as a Twitter or LinkedIn profile, to support their digital citizenship exploration. It was important to create a space for education leaders to experience similar tensions that their students might face in cultivating their own digital footprint. How could we teach our students about creating a purposeful digital footprint if we did not examine our own? This is the portion of the training that combined instructional goals with technical skills, but the goal was never to learn how to use specific tools or platform. Platforms will come and go, but the utility and design have remained the same since the inception of social media spaces.

At the conclusion of the session, I extended an optional and additional invitation for participants to post what they learned during their session. Many responses included how they had never considered their own digital footprint as an entry point into better understanding what it means to teach digital citizenship. Scan the QR code to view a participant's first post toward cultivating a digital presence with purpose as an education leader.

EXAMPLE PARTICIPANT TWEET

Moreover, the session helped school leaders recognize the necessity of digital citizenship instruction and left them hungry for more strategies to allocate resources and supports to further expand digital citizenship efforts.

Training for Change

There are system-level leaders who recognize the need for digital citizenship implementation, but are at a loss on where to begin or how to address across schools beyond selecting a curriculum and balancing the nuances of what digital citizenship means for diverse learners (Crompton, 2018; Rafalow, 2020; Watkins & Cho, 2018). This is where the ADKAR Model for change management (Hiatt, 2006) can support your systems-approach to creating professional learning for all digital citizenship levels. Consider digital citizenship learning opportunities as being designed on a continuum from sessions that help build awareness to professional learning experiences that offer new, fresh ideas for seasoned #DigCit leaders. Following are some examples of how to leverage a change management framework:

- Creating awareness can be in the form of Digital Citizenship Week (DCW). While this is not a traditional professional learning session, it remains an introductory pathway for stakeholders to develop digital citizenship awareness.
- Supporting the desire to participate can be in the form of empowering school leaders to consider the implications of their own digital footprint. The "Digital Presence with Purpose" example demonstrates a training session for school leaders to apply digital citizenship practices to their own identity as a leader, exploring their role in leading change across their school.
- Increasing knowledge and developing ability can be in the form of additional sessions designed internally according to personalized needs or inviting a partner to co-design a learning experience leveraging their propriety content. For example, to take our digital citizenship training for leaders to the next level, L.A. Unified partnered with KQED, an NPR-member news station based in

San Francisco, to offer media literacy training sessions. This partnership was born from keynoting at Facebook headquarters during the #DigCitCommit congress event held in February 2020. In having found alignment across our values and beliefs, it was a partnership the L.A. Unified team was eager to explore. Additionally, at this stage of change management where stakeholders are aware and eager to learn more, opportunities are ripe for asynchronous learning as well.

- Ensuring reinforcement can manifest in a cohort-style model of learning, where leaders who have advanced their digital citizenship knowledge and practices can support one another in their ongoing professional growth. This can also take the form of Twitter chats or other asynchronous learning opportunities.

Pushing a system through change is no easy task. It requires capacity-building at all levels with differentiated professional learning to support your system-level leaders and ensure the change effort has a strong foundation upon which to grow.

Chapter Wrap-Up

Policies, partnerships, and professional learning are vital components of a system-level digital citizenship program. Designing and maintaining such an effort requires engaging in a continuous improvement cycle, gathering input from key stakeholders while sharing and iterating on lessons learned. For example, at the onset of the pandemic, parents and legal guardians had to become all things—caretakes, teachers, and more—to their children forced to learn from home. An overwhelming need for digital citizenship supports for families was heard across the nation. Once a strong foundation and culture has been established around empowering digital citizenship practices, what other strategies does a Visionary Planner have to maintain such an initiative? We will explore this and throughout the rest of the book when policy becomes practice.

PART II

Implementation and Practice

In Part II, Carrie gives more specifics and strategies to take policy into practice. These chapters use case studies, past experiences, and expert advice on how to implement the ideas and goals of school and district leaders.

The Four-Frame organizational lens approach continues in Part II, with emphasis on the Symbolic frame. Policies are a starting place for systemic change, but policies alone cannot change school culture. Chapters 4 and 5 describe varying diverse perspectives from the school community and walk through steps on how to communicate and include everyone.

The last part of the book speaks to another important perspective in the school community: teachers. Chapters 6 and 7 describe strategies for adapting digital citizenship teaching to different ages and abilities, how to use the ISTE Standards in the classroom, and other advice from the field. Additional resources for educators and school leaders are found in the Appendix.

CHAPTER 4

Examining Perceptions and Deepening Inclusivity

People have different ways of addressing and conceptualizing the topic of digital citizenship, often depending on their culture, socio-economic group, and role in a school. This chapter will help the reader expand their own perceptions and challenge their assumptions about digital citizenship.

By the end of this chapter you will:

- compare and contrast different motivations and feelings behind digital citizenship with varying members of the school community
- understand different barriers of school participation and technology access
- reflect on your own assumptions, biases and feelings about digital citizenship

Avoiding a One-Size-Fits-All Approach

I (Carrie) vividly remember the first library story time I ever presented. Or rather, I remember clearly all the preparation for that first story time; the actual program was a bit of a blur. My first career was in public libraries when I was in my early 20s, a recent graduate with my master's in library science. Like many new graduates, I thought I knew more than I actually did. I had studied children's literature and how to put on a story time in library school, but at that point I had not actually run one. When preparing that first story time, I sat on the floor in front of a tall mirror, speaking out loud word for word what I would say throughout the whole story time. I practiced segues from a book to a song to an activity over and over again. I had written out in great detail what was essentially a script with a laboriously chosen theme and books that rested in my lap for reference. Through my late-evening rehearsals, I had memorized that entire script.

Educators reading this may remember their first time preparing a lesson—taking the theory of what they learned in school and applying it to the classroom. You may have written down each learning outcome or even made your own script. Then, once getting in front of students, you probably learned what I did—that my carefully detailed script was pretty worthless in action.

> Over the course of about 5 years as a youth services librarian, I put on more than 500 story times for different ages and abilities—and I only used a script that very first time.

I learned in that long-ago story time that even though I understood the theories of children's library programming and early literacy, the actual practice was different. Those theories treated young children in generic, generalized blocks, kind of like how economics treats consumers like rational decision makers who are keenly aware of the supply and demand curve. The children in my story time were not rational decision makers, and my age-appropriate titles did not appeal to all of them. Neither did my songs or my activities. Every child had different interests and attention spans. And even though the program was aimed at preschool ages, there was a wider developmental span in that library program room.

Over the course of about 5 years as a youth services librarian, I put on more than 500 story times for different ages and abilities—and I only used a script that very first time. I quickly learned that children are not one-size-fits-all and that I had to continually adapt and adjust each and every story time. Sometimes this would mean stopping my reading of a book, changing an activity last minute, or adjusting a craft. It would always mean knowing my audience and paying attention to the children in the room.

Unfortunately, in my work, I often encounter this one-size-fits-all, scripted approach to practicing digital citizenship. We as educators know from our experience that all students are different, yet we don't always treat them differently in our classrooms. We may stick to a script out of our own anxieties and lack of knowledge. Writing that script as a new librarian made me feel prepared, but it didn't prepare me in the way that working and interacting with children would. This chapter, and the rest of the book, describe those interactions. You'll read about the theory behind digital citizenship as well as about the (often messy) practice of implementation. You'll explore the different perceptions, biases, backgrounds, and assumptions around digital citizenship and how these things affect our understanding and practice of the concept.

Digital citizenship is a rapidly changing practice. Its relative newness, coupled with uncertainty about how to implement it and differing definitions on what it means, can cause anxiety and a lack of motivation in staff. That anxiety makes us want to stick to scripts or older ideas and programs that may be more familiar, but have often outlived their usefulness. This chapter describes the Symbolic frame of the Four-Frame Model in organizational behavior for school leaders referenced in Chapter 1, which "focuses attention on culture, meaning, belief, and faith. . . . Symbols govern behavior through shared values, informal covenants, and unspoken codes" (Bolman & Deal, 2019). By looking through the Symbolic frame lens, leaders can motivate and build a unified vision in digital citizenship.

Through case studies, on-the-ground experiences, and theory, this and the following chapters will help provide school leaders a more visible path from the clear roads of theory to the muddy and complicated trails of practice.

Considering All Perspectives in the Conversation

A person's perceptions create their reality—and, as discussed, there are varying perceptions around the multidisciplinary and broad topic of digital citizenship. It is difficult to create systemic change without including individuals and groups with different perceptions and coming to a common understanding of what that change might look like. School leaders must walk that fine line between listening to, empathizing with, and validating their staff while keeping to standards and policies.

> ## RELATED ISTE STANDARDS
>
> Students can play different roles in developing policy. They can share their experiences with stakeholders, help promote and bring awareness to the policy among the student body, and research what types of policies are in other schools and more. This chapter focuses on considering different perspectives and including all in the conversation. This global approach to learning and listening, which can help make policies and practices more inclusive, relates to the following ISTE Standard:
>
> **ISTE STANDARDS FOR STUDENTS: 1.7 GLOBAL COLLABORATOR**
>
> > 1.7.c Students contribute constructively to project teams, assuming various roles and responsibilities to work effectively toward a common goal.
>
> Chapter 4 also discusses the Symbolic frame, or how vision and culture affect our school community, which relates to the following ISTE Standard:
>
> **ISTE STANDARDS FOR EDUCATION LEADERS: 3.3 EMPOWERING LEADER**
>
> > 3.3.b Build the confidence and competency of educators to put the ISTE Standards for Students and Educators into practice.

They must incorporate school community members in their changes and decisions but not let their differing perceptions dictate the reality of the day-to-day mission and tasks of education.

Those (often vocal) groups and individuals who share their perceptions are important to listen to. But it's also vital to hear what's *not being said*, as many members of the school community do not have the same opportunities to express their thoughts and feelings. Based on the voices speaking out, school administrators may assume that the majority of a community perceives digital citizenship a certain way, when the input may instead reflect the views of a vocal minority.

This divide of opportunities and participation with marginalized groups is a result of many factors, including:

- **Transportation issues.** Community members may not be able to attend administration meetings or visit schools regularly because of a lack of reliable transportation.
- **Digital access.** If a community member does not have full digital access, they are less likely to know what's happening in a school, how to participate and share their thoughts, and more. While dedicated work in expanding digital access has increased in recent years, there are still swaths of the population without equitable access to technology. In the U.S., these access issues disproportionately affect lower income homes and families that are Black and/or Hispanic. Pew Research reports that 13% of adults in the U.S. with incomes below $30,000 do not have digital access at home. Black and Hispanic adults are less likely than white adults to have a traditional computer and home broadband (Atske & Perrin, 2021).
- **Distrust.** Community members may not trust the schools. This can be a result of prior negative experiences, feeling not listened to, and/or a distrust of government and institutions in general. Parents may distrust schools because they don't agree with what is being taught and feel the school pushes back on their beliefs. A distrust can also come from fear—community members may have different legal statuses. They may have dealt with systemic racism in schools. There are many reasons for distrust. But listening, reaching out, and validating those fears and distrust is an important step in regaining their trust.
- **Poverty culture.** Schools use formal vocabularies and have traditional (hidden) rules about decorum, navigating the system, and more. What do you wear when picking up your child? What are the different roles in the school and who do you talk to? These rules and conventions can alienate those who aren't part of the implicit middle-class culture of education (Payne, 2013).
- **Language barriers.** Community members may not speak the dominant language, or struggle with reading and writing. Schools may only send out communications in one language.
- **Time.** Many parents and caregivers hold multiple jobs and have multiple children. There are also single parents balancing a lot of responsibilities. The lack of time can mean less participation in school and community.
- **Emotional and cognitive resources.** A large-scale study published in *Science* found that poverty, and all the stresses it entails, imposed a mental burden similar to losing 13 IQ points. If an individual is continually stressed, they struggle

with long-term planning and decision-making (Mani et al., 2013). If a community member is stressed and only thinking about the day to day, why would they care about education policy? And if they did care, do they have the emotional resources to do something about it?

Case Study: Teaching Refugees

I saw these barriers to access in action during my experiences working with the refugee community in the Salt Lake City area, where I spent about a year and half teaching digital literacy to adult refugees at Salt Lake Community College. When teaching refugees, transportation and digital access can be significant issues. Fortunately, the education center was near public transportation, but my students would sometimes struggle to arrive on time in bad weather or on days with additional traffic. In terms of digital access, they all had some form of internet, but would mostly access the internet on smartphones. At the end of the six-month part-time digital literacy course, the adult students would receive a laptop. Those students had to regularly attend and participate in the class to receive the laptop. For some of them, it was the first they ever owned. Sharing devices across a household was common, and I remember several students asking me how to set up multiple accounts on the laptop since it would need to be shared across the whole family (Rogers-Whitehead, 2018a).

Later, my staff and I had opportunities to expand teaching to the Salt Lake refugee community through parent and student digital citizenship classes, which are still ongoing. Teaching digital parenting to refugees was unlike teaching parents at a private or charter school. These two parent groups' perceptions of digital citizenship differed, as did their needs in terms of access and support.

When I taught a group of refugee parents at a public housing complex, the class focused on digital literacy. They were unsure of the technology, how to manage settings, how to make purchases, and so on. Because of language and other barriers, these parents relied on their children to teach them how to use the devices. Sometimes that reliance led to struggles, such as an instance of a mother who realized her child had added her credit card to the smartphone and kept making purchases.

Contrast the desire in the refugee community for digital literacy and devices with parents from higher-income areas, who were often tech workers and had multiple devices for each member of the household. While many of the refugee parents were

TEACHING DIGITAL LITERACY TO REFUGEES

concerned with how to use the devices, the higher-income parents were concerned with how to limit them. This unique digital gap can be seen in hyperdrive in Silicon Valley. A backlash from affluent parents, there and in other affluent enclaves in the country, has created device-free preschools, parents requiring their nannies to prohibit all screens, and arguments with schools about online homework (Bowles, 2018).

I felt that backlash too when teaching digital parenting in higher-income areas. Some came to class wanting me to give stricter guidelines on screen time. I did not oblige. If a parent cannot articulate a reason for stricter guidelines and they simply lump all screen time into one category, then it's best not to be jumping ahead and making rules. Other parents attended the class less to learn and more to have an audience for their (very strong) opinions on technology. Meanwhile, when I talked with refugees in nearby communities, parents would describe the smartphone as an amazing technology to keep in touch with family around the world and a lifeline when they were in refugee camps (Rogers-Whitehead, 2018a).

While these two disparate groups of parents resided in nearby communities, sometimes even in the same district, their perceptions of technology diverged. Past experiences, language, culture, income, digital literacy skills, and more divided their outlook on digital citizenship and technology. Despite these differences, the goal of school leaders should not be reconciling this gap, but *understanding* it. That understanding, cultivated through talking and especially listening, can inform policy. A school leader who listens to the concerns not just of a vocal minority but of all parents from different incomes, backgrounds, experiences, and languages attains greater understanding and empathy. We often live in silos, going to school with those from similar neighborhoods, talking to people online who agree with us, and shopping and vacationing at the same places as those in our social class. This creates a gap in understanding of others' lived experiences. But for school leaders who listen to others outside their silos, they can address digital citizenship on multiple fronts—from digital access to digital safety.

Faith and Beliefs Around Digital Citizenship

A few years ago I had a conversation about the internet with an employee of The Church of Jesus Christ of Latter-day Saints (LDS) church, commonly known as the Mormon church (employees of the church are also active members). While the conversation was civil and positive, I keenly felt us both looking through different lenses on the subject of the online world. My lens was one of an educator, his was that of a faithful Latter-day Saint.

The conversation was wide-ranging, but it became clear we had different thoughts about internet filters. The LDS church has missionaries throughout the world—typically 18 or 19 years old—who proselytize, provide service, and work with local church members. Some can use a smartphone while on their mission, but phone usage is heavily monitored. A mobile device management tool is installed, other apps are blocked, and according to the church's handbook, missionaries are asked to "review each other's comments and messages before you post or send a message so that both of you can share ideas and be accountable for the outcome of the communication" (The Church of Jesus Christ of Latter-day Saints, 2021b). I was, and still am, uncomfortable with tracking and other filtering devices being used with adults, and I expressed that in the conversation. I feel adults should be empowered to make their own choices and digital identities. The Digital Citizen Advocate standard in the Coaches section of the ISTE Standards says it best with indicator 4.7.d, which states that coaches "empower educators, leaders and students to make their own informed decisions to protect their personal data and curate the digital profile they intend to reflect" (ISTE, 2020). How can a young person make their own decisions and create their own identity with constant monitoring?

> How can a young person make their own decisions and create their own identity with constant monitoring?

But while we didn't agree on that subject, I did gain some insight into the reason for those policies. These policies came from senior leadership in the LDS church and were guided by their faith. Technology was viewed through a different lens, as a potential positive but also as something that challenged religious faith. This belief is shared through a senior church leader's address to the LDS church during their semiannual conference in 2014: "The Internet provides many opportunities for learning. However, Satan wants us to be miserable, and he distorts the real purpose of things. He uses this great tool to promote doubt and fear and to destroy faith and hope" (The Church of Jesus Christ of Latter-day Saints, 2021a). But technology tools have also been a benefit to the LDS church. In our conversation, the employee also felt that technology had helped the missionaries reach potential converts and keep in touch with their families while they were away. We found common ground on this topic. We both recognized that while sometimes technology can be used to "distort," alternatively, it can also be a helpful tool to disseminate information across the world.

Building Empathy with Those with Disparate Values

It can be difficult to reconcile two different perceptions of technology. In this case, we had two different identities, or lenses, through which we viewed the same thing. And those identities may shift and change. An adult may view technology different when they become a parent. Someone who goes on a religious mission may see the internet differently when they are proselytizing and when they return home. But using the Symbolic frame of the Four-Frame Model and examining the values and beliefs behind the perceptions can develop empathy, kindness, and patience.

Table 4.1 illustrates how different members of the school community may talk about digital citizenship through the Symbolic frame. All have different motivations and words they use. A principal may be more interested in maintaining order. A parent may see technology as something that threatens their parental authority or disrupts family time. A teacher may see digital citizenship through standards and curriculum. All are valid viewpoints.

TABLE 4.1 Varying Views and Priorities of Digital Citizenship

	PRINCIPALS	PARENTS	TEACHERS
PRIORITY AND FOCUS	Policy	Religion/Faith	Curriculum
	Disciplining behavior	Desire for control	College and career readiness
	Politics and power	Emotions	Standards and outcomes

Being able to see different sides, hold multiple perspectives and identities, and listen with empathy is part of being a teacher and education leader. It's a hard balance, though, as leadership researchers Lee Bolman and Terrence Deal explain:

> *Teaching and learning are complex, and many of the toughest challenges—such as balancing caring and achievement or teaching as a science versus teaching as an art—are elusive. Every classroom is a miniature community, and each school is a distinctive culture. Trying to balance excellence, justice, and faith is an ongoing dance on a wobbly tightrope. But the moral obligation to attend to these intangible issues is the centerpiece of leadership. (Bolman & Deal, 2019)*

How do we identify different perceptions and values in others? One step is by looking inward at ourselves. Our identities inform the way we look at the world. We view the world through many lenses, most simultaneously. Some of those lenses, our identities, include:

- language
- nationality
- social class
- ethnicity
- sexual orientation
- race
- education
- ability status
- age
- family background
- religion

There's more than this list, of course, and diving deep into all these identities and more is beyond the scope of this book. But understanding where our perceptions originate can help school leaders when they are in the midst of heated discussions, feeling pressure from many sides, or just simply stressed when trying to implement change.

Examining Identity to Navigate Perceptions and Assumptions

The concept of positionality, a way of describing how an individual's identities shape their perceptions and understanding, is a framework to use when trying to bring people together for change, like when implementing digital citizenship. "All parts of our identities are shaped by socially constructed positions and memberships to which we belong" and are "embedded in our society as system" (Misawa, 2010). In a community or a classroom there are many shifting, fluid positions—and not all of those positions have an equal voice in trying to make change.

School leaders may find it helpful to think through their own identities, positions, and perceptions before talking to others. Some reflective questions for school leaders include:

- How do you identify yourself?
- How have your perspectives on your own identity changed over time?
- How do your identities shape your experience as a teacher, colleague, or administrator?
- How do your identities affect your beliefs about teaching and learning?

Starting by examining themselves, educators can learn to question their own perceptions that may be standing in the way of change, as well as their assumptions around technology. If someone has not struggled to use or access technology, they may assume others have had similar ease of use and access. Thoughts like "everyone should be able to understand this" or "all my students can watch this video at home" can hamper progress for digital learning and digital citizenship. With this in mind, ask yourself:

- What were my childhood experiences around technology? How did my family view technology?
- What was I taught, if anything, about technology in school?
- Have I ever struggled to access the internet?
- Have I ever done homework online?
- Have I ever been cyberbullied? If so, was I cyberbullied because of my race, gender, sexual orientation, or other identity?
- Am I a parent? If so, have I helped my child with online homework?
- Do I know how to troubleshoot issues online when they arise?

For a downloadable needs assessment tool to help both school leaders and classroom educators examine their perceptions of digital citizenship, scan the QR code.

This kind of self-reflection can then lead to a deeper understanding of members of the school community as well, with a recognition that different experiences and identities inform how we feel about technology and how we interact online. Religion is one lens that can affect our experience. In addition, students who identify as part of the LGBTQ+ community are more likely to be cyberbullied (ASPA, 2021). Someone who has been a victim of cyberbullying will likely have different perceptions of technology than one who has not. They may be wary to engage with new people online. Or they may get the impression that cyberbullying is something normal, and maybe even engage in it themselves.

In addition to examining their own approaches and perceptions, school leaders can model the actions they want to see from their students. As the Empowering Leader indicator 3.3.b of the ISTE Education Leader section states, leaders "build the confidence and competency of educators to put the ISTE Standards for Students and Educators into practice" (ISTE, 2018). School leaders set the vision of digital citizenship for educators—and their students—driving the creation of a culture in which it can thrive in the classroom. For example, the ISTE Student Standard Global Collaborator encourages students to "broaden their perspectives and enrich their learning by collaborating with others and working effectively in teams locally and globally" (ISTE, 2016). A demonstration of this

TOOLS FOR SCHOOL LEADERS

standard is having students participate in discussions in the school community. They can give their feedback on a policy and how they will celebrate Digital Citizenship Week. In this way, students can work to "broaden their perspectives" by talking, and most importantly, listening, to others who have different backgrounds and identities. As the Global Collaborator indicator 1.7.c of the Student section states, "students contribute constructively to project teams, assuming various roles and responsibilities to work effectively toward a common goal" (ISTE, 2016).

> If we aren't aware of people's experiences, we may think our experiences are universal. If we look through the world with one lens, we can't see through the other.

I know that teaching digital literacy to adult refugees years ago challenged my own assumptions. I had been online since I was a child and had used the internet for decades. Thus, I lapsed into what was normal and comfortable to me, using terms and jargon I assumed the class knew. Early on, I was confronted with my biases and assumptions when a student asked, "What do you mean a window?" I felt sheepish; I thought everybody knew what a computer window was.

Cognitive scientist Steven Pinker calls these assumptions the "Curse of Knowledge," the "difficulty in imagining what it is like for someone else not to know something that you know." He adds, "the inability to set aside something that you know but that someone else does not know is such a pervasive affliction of the human mind that psychologists keep discovering related versions of it and giving it new names" (Pinker, 2014). These might include egocentrism, hindsight bias, or mind blindness.

Whatever the name is, the idea remains the same. We make assumptions based on our knowledge or lack of knowledge. If we aren't aware of people's experiences, we may think our experiences are universal. If we look through the world with one lens, we can't see through the other. Pinker calls the Curse of Knowledge "insidious" and difficult to break. But he recommends that we "close the loop, as the engineers say, and get a feedback signal. . . . Only when we ask those people do we discover that what's obvious to us isn't obvious to them" (Pinker, 2014).

Chapter 6 will provide advice on communicating through different lenses—talking, and listening—to the community. But the first step is to examine yourself, and examine what vocabulary and language you are using in your community.

> ## CALIBRATING DEFINITIONS
>
> In Chapter 1, Vanessa describes her school district's experiences coming together on definitions of digital citizenship. Along with the definition of digital citizenship, they looked at reframing how it's addressed and what words were used. For example, they decided they wanted a proactive and empowering approach to digital citizenship, but their Acceptable Use Policy did not describe it properly. So they changed the wording in the Acceptable Use Policy to the Responsible Use Policy.

Finding a Shared Language

Every field has their own unique ways of communicating. This can be through acronyms, inside jokes, and/or heuristics or "mental shortcuts" ("Facebook is full of Boomers"). We communicate through these biases and shortcuts instinctively, and we don't often think, "What does that acronym mean spelled out?" or "What actually are the ages of people on Facebook?" When talking about digital citizenship, like other multidisciplinary subjects that involve many professions, these biases and styles of communication are often on full display. For example:

- using "digcit" instead of digital citizenship
- using online safety and digital citizenship interchangeably
- saying ISTE, instead of spelling it out
- using the word "standards" without specifying what type of standards, or where those standards come from

And a big one, assuming people actually know what "digital citizenship" is—and if they do say they know what it is, you both agree on the definition.

You're reading this book, so mostly likely you picked it with at least a basic understanding of the definition of digital citizenship. But you're most likely the exception, not the rule. Digital citizenship, that mouthful of a term, is still used mostly in books, academic discussions, conferences, articles, and think tanks. This process of finding agreed-upon definitions is also addressed in Chapter 1, and must also be addressed by school leaders when developing policy.

Check out the Google Search trends graph from the year 2021 (Figure 4.1). The jagged red line at the top is "online safety" and the blue one below is "digital citizenship." Furthermore, the top search query related to digital citizenship during that time frame is: "What is digital citizenship?" The second top search is "digital citizenship definition." Clearly, there's not only a lack of agreement on the definition of digital citizenship, but there's a lack of understanding of what the term really means.

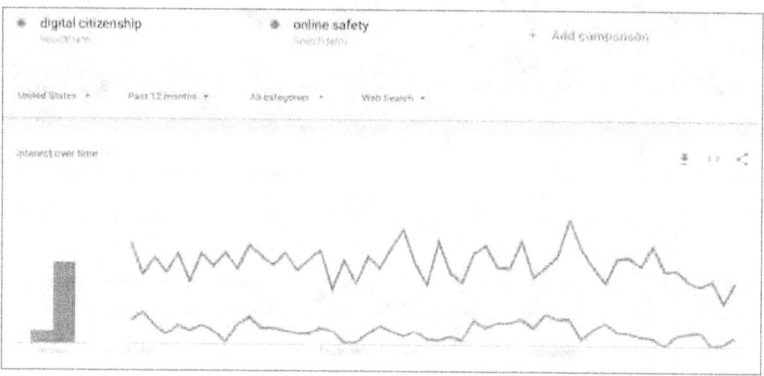

FIGURE 4.1 Google Search trends from 2021 illustrate how much more common the term "online safety" is than "digital citizenship," underscoring the need for more understanding around digital citizenship.

One way to achieve clarity around the meaning of these terms is through the ISTE Standards. Carolyn Sykora, senior director of ISTE Standards Programs, sees different definitions in digital citizenship and educational technology in general. "There's so many definitions out there that people come to the conversation with that background," she says. "It's kind of like *personalized learning*; there's a lot of different definitions. I think that creates confusion across the board. I think they are all valuable but have different lenses" (interview, September 2021).

Those different lenses come with different backgrounds and knowing those backgrounds can help build common ground.

Sykora recommends using the ISTE Standards to help with clarity around definitions. Those standards are built around skills and practice. "We're forced to create the standards as performance indicators: what they do, know or their disposition. It's written with a lot of verbs. . . . The more we can understand what are those essential practices, the more clarity we have in building those skills in those students and what we can expect in those discrete practices" (interview, September 2021).

But to get that clarity, people need to understand what standards are out there. Sykora notes, "There's still the huge swath of educators who don't know the standards." She recommends working to introduce the standards to change "hearts and minds" (interview, September 2021).

If school leadership wants to expand and scale digital citizenship, they need to go in with the assumption that most of the school community does not know what that phrase means, or has not even heard of the ISTE Standards. Perhaps in 5–10 years, that will no longer be the case, but who knows? What we do know for sure is that any kind of change management, campaign, or policy shift needs to not make assumptions about the definition of digital citizenship. And they shouldn't use those oh-so-comfortable mental shortcuts and jargons to describe the concept. If a school community remains stuck in theoretical debates on verbs and definitions, they can't get to actual practice.

Case Study: Teaching Youth in Custody

Digital citizenship is for everyone, but that doesn't mean everyone should have the same education in digital citizenship. We shouldn't use the same script. And we shouldn't use the same activities and examples. This is something I've experienced firsthand from working with the underserved.

In summer of 2021, my staff taught digital citizenship to a class of teens in state custody as part of their summer school program. It was a deep-dive program that ended in an assessment of knowledge and a post-survey. While some of the survey data had to be tossed out because students would come and go from custody during the class, over the course of the program, we found an increase in two important measures: their attitudes on their ability to keep themselves safe and their emotional awareness (Figure 4.2).

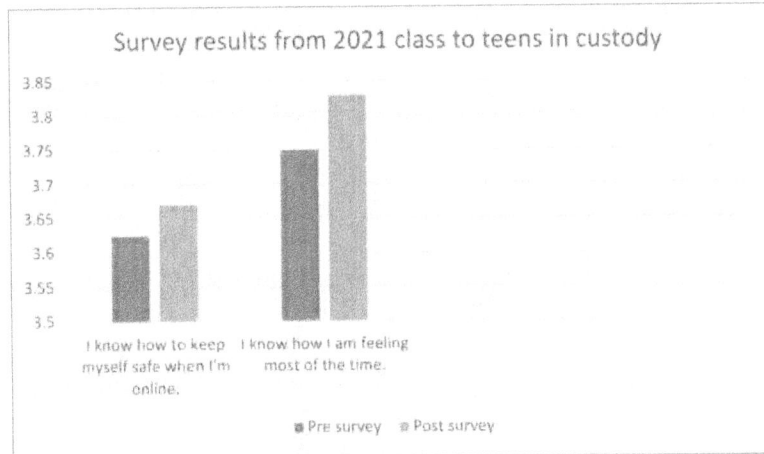

FIGURE 4.2
Students showed marked improvement in both ability to stay safe online and self-awareness from the beginning to the end of the program.

We had taught youth in custody before and found similar improvements. For example, in 2018 we taught a group of students who were even more interested in STEM and/or tech careers after taking the class. When we grasp the "whys" of technology through digital citizenship instruction, we can better understand the "hows" because it makes it easier to picture our future selves working in that space.

Students on the margins may not have had digital citizenship norms and behaviors reinforced at home. According to our surveys, all the teens in 2018 and 2021 had smartphones and internet access, but overall they lacked adult mentorship and guidance. Often their parents were in jail, or they were in foster care, or they simply bounced around often with little stability. More discussion of the "hows" and strategies of teaching digital citizenship inclusively will be covered in Chapters 5 and 7.

When these students are taught digital citizenship, overall they respond positively. While our surveys indicated some grumpiness about the assessment and preferences for some lessons over than others, students liked the classes. One teen wrote, "Thank you for the consistent positive attitude and interaction, also I appreciate the genuine personality and unconditional respect." That respect is a big piece when working to include differing perceptions and groups to scale and implement digital citizenship. And that respect should be for everyone, not just the vocal groups that show up to school meetings but also those that lack a voice, whether through limited digital access, language barriers, or being in a secure facility. That respect includes listening and self-reflecting on our own biases and perceptions. It also means looking up from our scripts and seeing who's directly in the room.

Chapter Wrap-Up

Chapter 4 covered people's different motivations, beliefs, and experiences that affect how they feel about digital citizenship. School leaders should work to understand other people's perceptions of digital citizenship and work to eliminate barriers of access, participation, and communication to implement changes in the school community.

The next chapter also discusses the importance of including the entire school community in digital citizenship efforts, particularly students with different abilities. It also provides learning strategies for educators on teaching digital citizenship to the neurodiverse and how technology can impact these individuals differently.

CHAPTER 5

Digital Citizenship for All Abilities

Scaling digital citizenship must include serving everyone in the school community. Inclusivity does not only mean making education available and suitable to different perceptions and experiences, it also includes adapting to learners of differing abilities. Like those from different backgrounds, individuals in the neurodiverse community are affected by technology in a variety of ways. Educators should adapt their teaching of digital citizenship to the biggest needs and most important skills to develop with neurodiverse students.

By the end of this chapter you will:

- be able to define the terms "neurodivergent" and "neurodiversity"
- understand the differing impacts of technology on those who are neurodivergent
- learn strategies for teaching digital citizenship to the neurodivergent

Teaching the Neurodivergent with Technology

In 2013, I (Carrie) received a Library Services and Technology Act (LSTA) grant to bring tablets into my library programming for individuals with high support needs. I saw technology as a tool to encourage developing social skills and motivating students. As you do in grant proposals, I cited many reference sources and wrote a *glowing* and *positive* account of the "amazing potential" tablets and software could have in my program. There were many positive results, but like with any idea turned to practice, the reality was more complicated. The tablets *did* motivate the students to work together on projects, transition to different activities, and manage behavior. But at the same time, the tech was a distraction and could exacerbate behavior issues just as much as mitigate them.

Technology is an impressive tool for students who think and learn differently than students who are neurotypical. This chapter covers many of those benefits. But it also discusses potential pitfalls and consequences of using technology in different learning environments. Technology does not affect everyone equally. The same remote learning that helped some students with functional needs thrive during the pandemic instead inhibited learning for others. Remote learning at home, unlike a day in a classroom, does not have the same routine, rules, and norms. In online leanring, there is a lack of consistency; familiar faces may not be present, the learning environment differs for each individual, and instructor reinforcement and support may not be as accessible. Impressive advances in adaptive technology have allowed more students to participate and communicate in class, yet like with my library program, that same technology can become an unhelpful distraction.

> Technology does not affect everyone equally. The same remote learning that helped some students with functional needs thrive during the pandemic instead inhibited learning for others.

Despite having classrooms of students whose bodies and brains vary widely, and on whom technology has different impact, educators often continue to teach digital citizenship as one-size-fits-all. They may all use the same lesson plans, or school leaders might put together an online safety assembly with the same message for every student.

RELATED ISTE STANDARDS

This chapter focuses on adapting and designing curriculum so students of all abilities can thrive and have their unique learning needs met. This approach to inclusivity relates to these ISTE standards:

ISTE STANDARDS FOR EDUCATORS: 2.5 DESIGNER

> 2.5.b Design authentic learning activities that align with the content area standards and use digital tools and resources to maximize active, deep learning.

ISTE STANDARDS FOR EDUCATION LEADERS: 3.3 EMPOWERING LEADER

> 3.3.b Build the confidence and competency of educators to put the ISTE Standards for Students and Educators in practice..

As discussed in the previous chapter, we take our values and perceptions into how we talk about and teach digital citizenship. It's already difficult to empathize with others' contrasting values, and it can be even harder when the person you're trying to understand literally has a brain that processes information differently than yours. Yet, we can still try, and we can still listen. This chapter shares experiences from working with neurodiverse students and brings their voices into the conversation. It provides teaching and talking tips to make digital citizenship education more inclusive so that learning can truly be for everyone.

Neurodiversity and Communication

"Neurodiversity" is a fairly new term originating out of the autism movement. It's a broad concept, just like digital citizenship, that encompasses differences in brain functioning including autism, ADHD, dyslexia, Tourette Syndrome, dyspraxia, and intellectual disability and can also be applied to mental health conditions and dementia. In this chapter, the word "neurodivergent" will be used to describe individuals whose neurocognitive functioning is not typical, while "neurodiverse" refers to a group of individuals, some of whom may be neurodivergent. The term "neurotypical" is used to describe those with typical neurological functioning.

Neurodiversity is a movement as well as a term. A big part of neurodiversity is advocacy which includes promoting the different varieties of neurocognition as positives and strengths, not deficits. For example, you'll read in this chapter the phrase "high support needs" rather than "low functioning." Jenara Nerenberg, the author of *Divergent Mind: Thriving in a World That Wasn't Designed for You*, writes about reframing the different ways people think and act:

> *The world will benefit significantly from talents such as empathy, emotional intensity, certitude, sensitivity, ability to detect details, depth of thought, will to embrace, and many other things that we need in a time where alienation, coldness, superficiality, and emotional hardness are dominating.* (Nerenberg, 2021)

The neurodiverse community seeks to change the language we use around intellectual disabilities and mental health. Some of those words and phrases, like "special needs" or "able-bodied," can be controversial (NCDJ, 2022). As shown in Table 5.1, another language change many in the neurodiverse community have suggested is shifting to a "identity-first" language rather than the medical model of "people first."

TABLE 5.1 People-First vs. Identity-First Language

PEOPLE-FIRST LANGUAGE	IDENTITY-FIRST LANGUAGE
"A person with dyslexia"	"Dyslexic person"
"Woman who is hard of hearing"	"Deaf woman"

Identity-first language emphasizes the disability, while people-first language emphasizes the person. For some neurodiverse people, they see their disabilities as central to who they are. Thus, being referred to as a "person with autism" may be perceived as condescending and/or erasing part of their identity (NJDC, 2022).

Sumiko Martinez, Director of the Autism after 21 Utah Initiative (scan the QR code to learn more), works with the neurodiverse community in the area of housing. Communication is a topic she has studied and an area she has worked in professional and academically. "Communication is everything," Martinez says, "and words are a big part of that. . . . For me, the language one uses comes down to a willingness to respect people" (interview, August 2021). This book primarily uses people-first language, but the reader should know that it's not the only way to refer to the neurodiverse community. When unsure—just ask.

AUTISM AFTER 21

"When you are working with communities around certain identities, ask people how they prefer to be identified," Martinez says, continuing, ". . . with autism spectrum disorder some people prefer to use identity-first language, such as 'autistic person,' and some prefer to use person-first language, such as a 'person with autism'" (interview, August 2021).

I know I have used older language in the past—and definitely made mistakes back in the early 2010s when I was learning about the neurodiverse community. I'm still learning how to improve my communication. I am also working harder to listen and learn from my students to make sure that digital citizenship lessons relate to their actual lived experiences. A big part of ensuring that all students feel welcome is humility. Martinez says, "You're going to make missteps sometimes. When you do, acknowledge it, apologize sincerely, and don't make that mistake again" (interview, August 2021).

Technology Use with People of Varying Abilities

Tay Gudmundson is a mother with attention deficit hyperactivity disorder (ADHD) who has children with "varying ADHD characteristics, compulsions and needs" (Digital Respons-Ability, 2022). She finds technology, particularly video games, both a "challenge and a break." With the way her brain operates, she has a desire to "game all day" because she says, "it is nice to not downward-spiral around decisions and how I'm going to accomplish tasks" (Digital Respons-Ability, 2022).

Overuse of technology is more of a symptom than a cause of behavior. Gudmundson, like many students, can find technology—whether through scrolling endlessly, watching YouTube video after video, or gaming all day—an escape from reality. The world is set up with routines, tasks, responsibilities, and assignments, and it can be stress-inducing. Technology is a way step away from anxieties, depression, stress, or struggles with executive dysfunction.

There is nothing wrong with using technology and media to take a break. According to research out of the University of Huddersfield, people who were "rife with anxiety" turned to TV to relieve stress during the early months of the pandemic (Johnson & Dempsey, 2020). It's no surprise that viewing went up overall during the stress of the spring 2020 lockdowns, particularly with the ease of access to streaming services and YouTube (Johnson & Dempsey, 2020).

However, a break can quickly turn into a pattern, then a hard-to-break habit. And it's hard to know how much is too much, how long of a "break" one needs, and what habits can create negative consequences and impairments. Authors of a research article in *Frontiers in Psychiatry* discussed the debate and research in this area. "Initial evidence indeed suggests that binge-watching may represent an emerging addictive behavior which is reflected in individuals' loss of control over watching time, impairment of day-to-day functioning, sleep quality and social relationships" (Boursier et al., 2021).

Everyone has different methods to cope. Some are just healthier than others. When a coping method decreases social interaction, isolates the person, affects their grades or paid work, significantly decreases physical activity, or impacts sleep—then the coping mechanism has hurt more than helped. Whether the "break" of increased media consumption is healthier or harmful depends on the individual's motivation.

> When a coping method decreases social interaction, isolates the person, affects their grades or paid work, significantly decreases physical activity, or impacts sleep—then the coping mechanism has hurt more than helped.

The researchers in the *Frontiers in Psychiatry* article looked at samples of people with differing motivations for their increased television viewing. Those who consumed more TV for coping and escapism were more likely to lose control and binge watch. Others who watched for "pleasure deriving from positive emotions and relationships," such as those who watched shows with friends or wanted to learn more about a topic, typically watched for fewer hours. Those positive emotions and relationships were a protective factor against unhealthy media consumption. The authors write: "Particular attention should be paid to the motivations underlying binge-watching and its potential consequences" (Boursier et al., 2021).

REMOTE LEARNING AS AN OPTION, NOT JUST AN ACCOMMODATION

Schools were forced to provide remote learning during the pandemic, whereas in the past this kind of accessibility option was provided only at the school's discretion and interpretation of "reasonable accommodations." For colleges that offered classes online during the pandemic with discounts on tuition, it was difficult to argue that remote learning is "fundamentally different from, or inferior to, in-person instruction" (Morris & Anthes, 2021). This meant more students at the K–12 and higher-ed levels had opportunities for remote learning than ever before.

Remote learning in some ways levels the playing field among students in a classroom. Students with disabilities are not an "other" or an "exception" with remote options (Morris & Anthes, 2021). They can work around medical appointments, log in to a waiting room, and have more flexibility in participation. The social component of remote learning can also be a benefit for students with social anxieties or challenges around communication. They are less likely to be distracted or uncomfortable in a classroom and less likely to be bullied in person, although online bullying is still a potential issue. Remote learners also may feel more comfortable typing a response than verbalizing it.

Not all students with ADHD benefitted from remote learning, however. One study out of the *Journal of Adolescent Health* found that in the short term, adolescents "had more remote learning difficulties," while noting that those who had less regular routines were more negatively impacted (Becker et al., 2020). The increased flexibility and decreased structure of remote learning was a benefit for some students with ADHD and a detriment to others.

Even as most students have returned to in-person learning, remote learning is increasingly an option, not just a necessary accommodation. For many students, it may be their preferred and best choice for learning long after the pandemic is over.

Individuals who are neurodivergent, whether with ADHD, autism, or various mental health disorders, have increased risk factors that can lead to unhealthy digital behaviors like binge-watching or doomscrolling. Some of those risk factors include:

- **Bullying.** A 2017 report from the U.S. Department of Health and Human Services 46.3% of adolescents with autism spectrum disorder were victims of bullying. That is substantially higher than adolescents that are neurotypical (U.S. Department of Health and Human Services, 2017).

- **Dopamine functions.** Dopamine is a neurotransmitter that helps brain cells communicate over short distances. It also has a role in motivation and addiction related to its ability to help people feel pleasure and reward. Many mental illnesses are linked to low levels of dopamine, and dopamine deficits and imbalances are related to other disorders such as autism, ADHD, Tourette's, and dyspraxia (Kirby, 2021).

- **Executive functioning.** Executive functioning, also known as higher-brain functioning or cognitive control, is typically different in those who are neurodivergent. For example, "ADHD patients have deficits in higher-level cognitive functions necessary for mature adult goal-directed behaviors" that, according to research, is caused by a variety of factors such as impairments in certain areas of the brain, delays in cortical thickness and less volume of gray and white matter in the brain (Rubia, 2018). ADHD and autism commonly coexist, particularly with children and while more research is needed, both disorders have executive function deficits and may share a common genetic basis (Leitner, 2014).

For an individual with deficits in executive functioning and dopamine, technology is a near-irresistible temptation and distraction. They may get an increased amount of dopamine for their activities online compared with someone who is neurotypical. They also may struggle with time management, making plans, and more due to their executive dysfunction. And due to an increased risk of bullying, they may turn to technology to cope. All these risk factors make it difficult to put down their devices and can slowly lead them into unhealthy digital habits.

Digital citizenship education is needed more for individuals who are neurodivergent. They are more likely to be behind screens longer because of their executive function issues that make it harder to self-regulate. Also, being online and not dealing with face-to-face interactions can feel calming and safe to them. But that additional time online does increase their risk of cyberbullying, grooming, and other online safety issues. They also struggle with decision making and planning, which means that concepts of digital health and wellness, creating balance between technology and life, are vital. For people who have executive functioning concerns, they may struggle with social cues, meaning that digital communication can be fraught. This means digital structures, rules, and routines are important both at school and home.

Table 5.2 summarizes these risk factors and how technology can both benefit and detract. Digital citizenship education is a powerful tool to address the potential risk factors for those whose brains function differently than those of neurotypical people.

TABLE 5.2 Pros and Cons of Technology Use by the Neurodiverse

RISK FACTORS	PROS OF TECHNOLOGY	CONS OF TECHNOLOGY	HOW DIGITAL CITIZENSHIP EDUCATION CAN HELP
Cyberbullying	There are online communities that can make students feel safe and supported.	Increased tech use comes with increased potential for being a victim of cyberbullying.	Instruction on what to do when you're being cyberbullied and how to change settings can help prevent cyberbullying.
Dopamine functions	Technology can give a dopamine boost and sense of purpose and pleasure.	The positive dopamine boost can create feedback loops where individuals need more and more dopamine to feel well.	Teaching on self-awareness can help students monitor their emotions and understand how technology use impacts those emotions.
Executive functioning	There are many productivity tools to help individuals focus, including apps for mindfulness, timers, reminders, calendars, and more.	The free-form flexibility of the online space and endless potential for stimulation makes it hard for some to focus and plan ahead.	A part of digital citizenship is digital wellness. This type of instruction can help students learn to balance and manage their own tech use.

Over the years Gudmundson learned that if she has too much screen time it will "lead to boredom and feeling irritable. So, I have specific periods of time during the day when I game" (Digital Respons-Ability, 2022). She also implements those rules for her children.

> When my kids get home from school, they're allowed 30 minutes on the Switch or iPod to decompress. Then it's time for household tasks, friends, dinner, then bedtime. Our family has to have this structured routine. It's something my children rely on. Having definite end times with timers teaches them that there is a time and place for gaming. Days when we do not help them with these boundaries on their time are days that end in tears and chaos. (Digital Respons-Ability, 2022)

Educators can take some of the experiences of Gudmundson's family into their own classroom and establish their own rules and routines. Later in this chapter, we'll share more details and strategies for how to adapt and teach digital citizenship to those with varying abilities, such as ADHD.

THE POSITIVE SIDE OF GAMEPLAY

Video gaming, like remote learning, is another use of technology that has the potential to be of great benefit to neurodivergent individuals. A 2014 study in *Cyberpsychology, Behavior and Social Networking* found that online gaming is advantageous to emotionally sensitive individuals in making friendships (Kowert et al., 2014). These virtual spaces were places where they could have an avatar, a character or identity that feels safe and comfortable to them. They were also places where they could communicate more freely, without missing nonverbal physical cues, as well as having extra time to prepare a response.

Recent research that studied gameplay during the pandemic found a small positive correlation with gameplay. Using industry data along with player self-reporting, the authors write: "Our results advance the field in two important ways. First, we show that collaborations with industry partners can be done to high academic standards in an ethical and transparent fashion. Second, we deliver much-needed evidence to policymakers on the link between play and mental health. More research on the effects of gaming is needed, but there is the potential that for some individuals of different abilities they can be a positive and safe place in their lives" (Johannes et al., 2021).

Case Study: Teaching Digital Citizenship at a State Hospital

This past summer I taught digital citizenship and digital literacy for two weeks at a secondary school within a secure facility: the Utah State Hospital. In the class were neurodiverse students, including those with autism, ADHD, and mental illness. Most likely, these students had multiple conditions because there is "extensive evidence that greater rates of depression and anxiety" co-occur "with autism, dyspraxia, and ADHD. For example, nearly 3 in 10 children diagnosed with ADHD have an anxiety disorder" (Rubia, 2018). Comorbidity of anxiety is even higher with autism, with some studies finding up to 84% of young people with autism suffering from anxiety (Rogers-Whitehead, 2020).

I loved teaching those classes. The students were very bright, and we had some deep discussions. At the end of the classes the students took a test of their knowledge, and most did very well. And from their anonymous surveys taken before and after the class, I believe they enjoyed it too, with one middle schooler describing the class as "fun and helpful."

But while I enjoyed teaching the students, I had to be quick on my feet and ready to pivot and adapt at every turn. I also learned a lot. If I were to advise another person, or teach digital citizenship to these classes again, here are my recommendations:

- **Keep the lessons moving.** Many of these students had ADHD or other conditions that affected their attention span. I found I needed to speed up my lessons, intersperse them more with stories and anecdotes, and not spend too long on just one topic.

- **Keep a professional distance.** When I started working with youth in secure care facilities years ago, I had to take a training that addressed the topic of manipulation. Many of these young people have been groomed, manipulated, and abused themselves (Timmerman & Schreuder, 2014), and sometimes they engage in similarly unhealthy behaviors to gain favor from the adults in the facility. When working in these spaces, be aware that individuals may praise you or try to gain confidence by giving a gift or saying something like "You're the only one that makes a difference around here" or complimenting clothes or hair.

- **Understand their relationships to technology.** To the survey question "Where do you keep your phone at night?" one male teen responded, "In my head." That response stayed with me. Many young people who struggle with mental illness may be isolated from peers, bullied, or rejected, but their phone can be a lifeline to another place. It can be a space where they feel freer to speak up and be themselves, and to be listened to. In the hospital, these teens were not allowed to have personal internet-connected devices, which elicited some complaints during the classes.

- **Provide a distraction.** These neurodivergent students struggled to focus for very long. Part of this was medication. A few times when teaching a morning class, I had students that could barely stay awake, and a couple of times one fell asleep. Some of the medication used to treat their conditions made them tired. They also struggled with sleeping at night, some needing additional medication. Throughout every class I provided paper, a workbook that supported the lessons, coloring pages, and markers. The ability to draw or color kept them more focused on the lessons. One student remarked in their survey that "drawing while learning" was their favorite part.

- **Be careful with supplies.** I was warned before teaching these classes not to have any staples in my workbooks because they could be used for harm. So, I removed the staples and used rubber bands to hold the books together. It immediately became clear that was a mistake. Rubber bands were used to self-harm, to flick at others, and as a distraction for a few students who quickly scooped up their classmates' rubber bands. Many students were not happy when the rubber bands were confiscated, and one noted on their survey that their "least favorite activity" in the class was taking away the rubber bands.

During the classes I also surveyed the hospital staff who were a mix of teachers and psychiatric aides. When asked about issues with technology with the students, the staff listed:

- **"Behaviors, mental illness, processing."** The processing referred to were issues with executive functioning, like thinking long-term. One of the lessons taught was about college and career and applying for jobs—which elicited less interest than other courses. Some of the students struggled to think that far ahead and wondered why they even needed that information.

- **"Pay attention to where they are going online—stop just clicking on items to get where the student wants to go."** I asked for more details from this staff member on this response, and they said that students often didn't even look at the website, they just started clicking. They didn't have search skills—or the patience to learn or demonstrate those skills. This lack of patience may relate to those executive dysfunctions.

"Inappropriate computer use; not understanding the dangers online."
This feedback is common from teachers—all students struggle with understanding the dangers online. But students who are neurodivergent, particularly with autism, may lack social cues and awareness that can provide red flags and get them to step back and reflect. Those who are neurodivergent and socially isolated may also be at risk for manipulation. These students, like all students, want to feel loved and accepted and someone with malicious motives can more easily take advantage of that desire.

Digital citizenship is not one-size-fits-all. When teaching these classes I learned quickly which digital citizenship subjects had more value to the students (sleep and technology, online safety) and which ones didn't (college and career). I learned to shorten my lessons and lengthen the time for them to do activities and take their tests. Diagnostic tools and awareness have meant that more students have a diagnosed mental illness than in generations past. They are very likely to be in your classroom. What exactly does that mean as these students interact with technology?

> Diagnostic tools and awareness have meant that more students have a diagnosed mental illness than in generations past. They are very likely to be in your classroom. What exactly does that mean as these students interact with technology?

A school leader's role in this is to support this flexible and adaptive learning. This may mean providing a budget for more sensory activities or professional learning for educators, and it may mean coming into some of these physical or online classrooms so they can see the reality of teaching these neurodiverse learners. The Empowering Leader Standard of the Education Leaders section of the ISTE Standards addresses this in indicator 3.3.d: "Support educators in using technology to advance learning that meets the diverse learning, cultural and social-emotional needs of individual students" (ISTE, 2018).

Case Study: Mental Illness and Technology Use

There has been a great deal of talk and concern about the link between adolescent mental health and technology. American psychologist and author Dr. Jean Twenge has been a leading voice on the topic, along with many individuals and organizations including the Center for Humane Technology and the CEO of Common Sense Media Jim Steyer. These discussions were ignited again in late 2021 with Frances Haugen, who supplied Congress with files from Facebook and testified that Facebook knew that their systems and algorithm harmed vulnerable people, like teens on Instagram (Ortuary & Klepper, 2021).

There is legitimate bipartisan anger toward the Facebook leak, and there is an increase in adolescent mental health issues. But does technology actually *cause* these issues? Is it just a correlation or causation?

School leaders are faced with this issue, through upset parents, bad press of online incidents in their districts that may go viral, and fears and anxieties of their staff. It can be hard to lead in a highly volatile system with strong emotions, but the ISTE Standards for Education Leaders provide one guide. Empowered leaders spread confidence, not worry. They should "build the confidence and competency of educators to put the ISTE Standards for Students and Educators in practice," according to indicator 3.3.b (ISTE, 2018).

> Empowered leaders spread confidence, not worry. They should "build the confidence and competency of educators to put the ISTE Standards for Students and Educators in practice," according to indicator 3.3.b (ISTE, 2018).

In a systemic review of changes between technology engagement and mental health through three nationally representative samples, research published in *Clinical Psychological Science* in 2021 found mixed results. According to their research, the authors write, "technology engagement had become less strongly associated with depression in the past decade, but social-media use had become more strongly associated in emotional problems." Other changes in mental health and associations in technology were not found. The researchers conclude that there is "little evidence for increases in the associations between adolescents' technology engagement and mental health" (Appel et al., 2019).

Other reviews of literature have found more correlations between technology use and mental health (Appel et al., 2019). But the link is still unclear because there are more variables (e.g., race, gender, age socioeconomics, preexisting conditions) than just technology. It's hard to separate a person from those preexisting conditions. People don't use technology in a vacuum; it's usually a social activity, done in different environments by people with varying backgrounds and genetics. Still, no research at the time has conclusively proved a causal claim that technology use leads to negative (or positive) mental health (Appel et al., 2019). Like with research around increased TV viewing during the pandemic, technology *use* is more of a symptom than a cause. The researchers in the *Clinical Psychological Science* study write, "In fact, some longitudinal studies have found the opposite, whereby mental health problems predict smartphone use rather than phone use predicting mental health problems" (Appel et al., 2019).

More research needs to be done on this topic because the technology being blamed, including streaming services, YouTube, and social media, is still new. Longitudinal data, and not just static self-reports, are needed. Dr. Markus Appel and his co-authors write,

> *A more accurate understanding of how children and young people are affected by new technologies would be enabled by studying their effects over time. But because researchers have assumed that technology effects are fixed, at least two time-dependent changes have evaded systematic testing.*
>
> *First, when fears emerge about a new technology, worries about previous technologies are largely abandoned without an agreement on—or good data indicating—whether, why, or how the previous technologies were or were not harmful. In a stepwise fashion, focus is instead redirected to the new technology of concern, along with the suggestion that it is more harmful because of technological advancement. Because interest moves elsewhere, there are few or no tests of whether the effects of previous technologies . . . actually increased or decreased as society's attention shifted to the possible harms associated with more recent technologies (e.g., playing video games).* **Therefore, we have not learned how existing technologies' effects change as new technologies emerge and are adopted by young people.** *(Appel et al., 2019)*

Technology has always been a scapegoat for society's ills—and from the radio to the automobile to the television, it has often led to feelings of blame and anger (Rogers-Whitehead, 2021). Anger, and its close counterpart, fear, do not help foster education and awareness. Anger may get more parents to attend digital citizenship-related events and even politicians to fund more programs. But fear and anger do not create good policy and practice. Technologies come and go quickly, igniting the news cycle and then dying down. As educators, we should not jump on the latest media trends or the political outrage machine. So what *should* we do to address these kinds of concerns?

What Can Educators Do?

When I was a librarian, I created the first library program for young people with autism in the state. And when I started, I didn't know what I was doing. I relied on a wonderful volunteer, professionals, parents, and more when finding how to adapt my existing library programs to support the needs of those on the autism spectrum. The experiences and quotes from some of the great people who helped me are featured in my book *Serving Teens and Adults on the Autism Spectrum: A Guide for Libraries* (Rogers-Whitehead, 2020). Scan the QR code for more information about the book, resources, and a free downloadable guide on making spaces more inclusive.

SERVING TEENS AND ADULTS ON THE AUTISM SPECTRUM

In that book, I share a story from my early days of learning about autism. While touring a special education classroom with an educator and watching the students work, I asked her what she and other teachers focused on for these students. She listed three skills: teamwork, transitions, and social skills (Rogers-Whitehead, 2020). In this section, I'll elaborate on these skills through a digital citizenship lens. While I don't run my library programs for people on the spectrum anymore, I still work with neurodivergent individuals and continue to keep in mind those three soft skills (Table 5.3).

For young people who are neurodivergent, some digital citizenship concepts and competencies have a greater impact than others. This section will discuss best practices from the field on how to teach those topics.

TABLE 5.3 Key Skills for Neurodivergent Students Through a Digital Citizenship Lens

DIGITAL CITIZENSHIP LENS	TEAMWORK	TRANSITIONS	SOCIAL SKILLS
Related soft skills	Cooperation and collaboration	Self-regulation	Communication and empathy
Digital citizenship concept	Digital communication, digital advocacy	Digital health and wellness	Digital communication and digital etiquette

UDL AS A GUIDE

When discussing adapting digital citizenship teaching and learning, educators should look at Universal Design for Learning (UDL) as a guide. UDL is often used to support students who are neurodivergent or have differing abilities. One application of UDL is about designing curricula that has multiple means of engagement, multiple means of representation, and multiple means of action and expression (CAST, 2018).

How could UDL be applied in digital citizenship education? One example would be using self-assessments and reflection after discussing digital ethics (means of engagement). Another possibility is creating digital goals in class as part of a series of digital citizenship lessons (means of action and expression). If teaching digital citizenship online, educators can provide written transcriptions, diagrams, videos, and multiple forms of auditory and visual media to support the student (means of representation).

UDL is a detailed concept and beyond the scope of this book, but to learn more, scan the QR code to check out the full Universal Design for Learning Guidelines on the CAST website.

UDL GUIDELINES

Self-Regulation and Transitions

When I've trained librarians about serving individuals on the autism spectrum, I ask them the question, "How do you self-regulate?" The term "self-regulation" can be conflated with *coping*—and technology is a popular way to cope or self-regulate. In response to the question, librarians have sometimes described coping through technology with activities like bingeing Netflix, or without technology by knitting. Sometimes people pause when they hear the question. They may not even be aware of how or if they are doing it. I know I do it. For example, I have a tendency to hum in certain situations—and I don't always even realize I'm making noise until I get a funny stare. We all self-regulate, just in different ways.

> Self-regulation is related to the ability to transition from one task to another. It's an essential skill not only for being a digital citizen but also for college and career success.

While I sometimes self-regulate through humming, students with different abilities may self-regulate in more overt and sometimes even harmful ways. Individuals on the autism spectrum are more likely to self-harm (i.e., biting, skin-picking, cutting, head banging) than those with other conditions (Haddock & Hagopian, 2020). The ability to self-regulate for many who are neurodivergent is not just a means for academic success, but for their own physical health. When compared to some of those behaviors, bingeing Netflix is a more positive option.

Self-regulation is related to the ability to transition from one task to another. It's an essential skill not only for being a digital citizen but also for college and career success. At work and school, people need to be able to switch over to different tasks rapidly. If a person struggles with switching tasks, it impacts their productivity, and for those who are neurodivergent those transitions can be upsetting and confusing. Neuropsychologist Dr. Michael Rosenthal calls this struggle with transitioning in young people with autism and ADHD "cognitive inflexibility" (Martinell, 2021). Technology adds another layer to the difficulties in transitioning. There's a lot of information thrown at us online. Media online can be overstimulating, and if a student is easily stimulated, transitioning can seem sudden. This sudden shift can upset them because they don't feel like they have control of their environment (Martinell, 2021).

Digital health and wellness is a part of digital citizenship. The teaching of digital wellness concepts, such as balancing screen time, not letting technology impact sleep, the ability to self-reflect, and being emotionally aware, are both *harder* and *more important* for individuals with differing abilities. Their executive dysfunctions, dopamine functions, and comorbidity for other conditions makes them struggle with self-regulation. But those same conditions mean that technology may be a *healthier* way to self-regulate than other ways. Using technology has fewer physical health effects than other coping behaviors, such as self-harm, binge-eating or purging, or substance abuse.

Some strategies for educators to teach digital wellness, and digital citizenship in general, for those that may have struggle with self-regulating include:

- **Be careful when talking about screen time.** Do not lump all screen time into one category, but rather, treat it as a spectrum, as diverse as the students you're working with. Withhold judgement on these students' use of screens. Have an activity where you have the students share both their screen and non-screen hobbies and activities.

- **Include sensory activities.** When I taught at the state hospital, I allowed students to draw the entire time. It was a means of self-regulating and helped them focus and pay attention. But sometimes items to fidget can cause them to pay less attention (i.e., the rubber band problems; see the case study at the beginning of this chapter), so choose wisely. Some other sensory/fidget activities I've included in digital citizenship classes are:
  - putty
  - adult coloring books
  - digital citizenship coloring pages

Note: Scan the QR code to download a free copy of a fidget book I created to provide sensory activities and reinforce the lessons in my digital citizenship classes. More examples are also available on this book's companion site.

FIDGET ACTIVITY BOOK

- **Give a cue for transitions.** Being able to self-regulate, to redirect and refocus, means it's easier to move from one task to another. Consider having a song, rhyme, certain sets of words, lights dimming, or some other kind of sign when it's time to move on to something else.

- **Limit tabs and online distractions.** If teaching digital citizenship online, try to limit distractions. Just the fact that the course is online and you have less control over the environment can make this tough. Apple products have the Guided Access feature that can temporarily restrict the user from moving to other tabs; Google's Digital Wellbeing has similar functions. Learning management systems also have locking or proctoring mechanisms to restrict activities outside the platform.
- **Suggest alternative self-regulating tools.** We all need multiple ways of self-regulating. It's hard to simply stop one habit without any kind of substitution or environmental change. Expecting students to just stop picking at their skin or being online too much is unrealistic. Environmental change, not just willpower, is also needed. This means one needs to take a step beyond the desire to change to an actual physical tweak or adjustment. For example, wearing a long shirt to cover up the skin, or using a screen time app to moderate online time are both examples of a physical step toward change.
- **Teach in smaller groups.** Teaching digital citizenship in an assembly, or primarily through lecture, does not provide multiple means of engagement and representation (discussed in the "UDL as a Guide" sidebar). Large groups can also be uncomfortable for some students, creating a sensory overload and other factors. In smaller groups, students may feel more comfortable expressing themselves, and they have more chances to speak and fewer distractions from their peers' noises and movements.

Teamwork and Social Skills

Most humans are experts in nonverbal communication. We can quickly glance at a colleague or family member and have a pretty good guess what they're thinking. Newborns' eyes are immediately attracted to faces and can pick out their caregiver's voices even if they don't understand the words.

But for those who have sensory processing issues, picking up nonverbal messages is harder. Their brains take in more input from the world. This means all stimuli from a social situation—eye movements, gestures, unspoken expectations, etc.—can be overwhelming.

Digital communication presents both a challenge and an opportunity for those who struggle with social skills. On one hand, communicating online, like through a game, can feel positive and safe. They may feel more relaxed in these spaces because their brain isn't trying to sift through all the input it's rapidly receiving. On the other hand, being able to interpret and communicate nonverbal cues is a very important skill. One famous study in 1970 had subjects analyze the nonverbal cues in video tapes and found that the nonverbal cues had 4.3 times the effect of verbal cues (Argyle et al., 1970). Being able to understand nonverbal cues is important for healthy relationships, academic and career success, and better understanding the world in general.

> Being able to understand nonverbal cues is important for healthy relationships, academic and career success, and better understanding the world in general.

If a person struggles to interpret nonverbal cues face-to-face, this also means they may struggle online. Nonverbal cues are implicit; they aren't written down and explained. No one tells you when you're growing up what exactly a raised eyebrow or downward shift of the mouth means. But these unspoken facial cues spell out unwritten rules. And if you can't understand the nonverbal cues, you are missing out on the social and cultural norms, or rules. The internet is full of unwritten rules. An emoji, just like a raised eyebrow, can convey multiple meanings. Different online platforms have different cultures and norms. They are full of inside jokes, unspoken taboos, and sometimes overzealous moderators and commentors who strictly reinforce those norms. Someone who does not understand the nonverbal cues and unwritten rules is like a traveler in a foreign country without a map.

This struggle can be an online safety concern. Someone who is neurodivergent may not know if a corporation, or unscrupulous person, is preying upon them. They may inadvertently hurt others through their words or misinterpret someone else's messages. They may struggle to critically evaluate media that may try to persuade or influence them. The inability to communicate is a risk factor for many issues. The Centers for Disease Control and Prevention (CDC) lists individual, peer, and community risk factors linked to youth violence (CDC, 2020). These are not direct causes, but young people who experience these risk factors are more prone to being either a victim or a perpetrator of violence. Some of these risk factors that are related to being neurodivergent and/or struggling with communication include:

- attention deficits, hyperactivity, or learning disorders
- poor behavioral control
- deficits in social cognitive or information-processing abilities
- high emotional distress
- social rejection by peers

Encouraging social skills and teamwork through digital communication learning is not just a digital health and wellness issue, but one of online safety. As noted before, those with autism are high risk for being bullied (U.S. Department of Health and Human Services, 2017). Depression and anxiety are more common in individuals with ADHD or autism which can mean that if they are bullied, rejected, or isolated, the distress hits them harder. This can create a vicious cycle with digital behavior. The more they are rejected, they turn online, but being online more is a risk factor for more rejection.

> Encouraging social skills and teamwork through digital communication learning is not just a digital health and wellness issue, but one of online safety.

So, what can educators do to help teach and encourage these important digital citizenship concepts of healthy digital communication and etiquette? How can educators be a true Designer and model the ISTE indicator 2.5.b to "design authentic learning activities that align with the content area standards and use digital tools and resources to maximize active, deep learning"?

- **Teach digital empathy.** When we cannot see the other person and pick up those nonverbal cues online, we may struggle to feel empathy for them. Research published in *Computers in Human Behavior* found that adolescents with lower empathy were both more likely to cyberbully and be cyberbullied by others. Empathy-based interventions are suggested to address these behaviors (Brewer & Kerslake, 2015).

- **Use social stories.** Social stories are used with students on the autism spectrum to help them know what to do in social situations. But they can be used with all students to help them role-play and be empathetic to others. Social stories can be used with any subject, including what happens online. Research has found social stories are more effective if they are visual (Kokina & Kern, 2010). Consider these visual activities to role play and self-reflect:
    - **Create comic book stories.** Developed by Carol Gray for those with autism spectrum disorder, these comic strips are visual representations of what was being said in a conversation, how people might be feeling, and their motivations and/or intentions in the conversation.
    - **Tell stories with emoji.** Use common emoji symbols to tell social stories and ask the students what they mean. Doing this can not only teach basic emoji, but also give an opportunity to demonstrate how one symbol can be interpreted in different ways.
- **Encourage observation and listening.** The internet has allowed us all to be spectators to countless conversations going on at one time on all manner of platforms. Pick a few and discuss what was being said, as well as what was *not* being said. You can also encourage such observations for real-life conversations. Two students can talk, and another can observe and share what they interpreted from the conversation.
- **Teach digital etiquette.** Spend additional time teaching digital etiquette. These rules of etiquette are not always explicit and can change in different contexts. For those who struggle with social skills, the rules of etiquette can be particularly tricky. When teaching digital etiquette, spend extra time addressing what to say in different contexts (i.e., on different platforms, to different people, etc.). See the lesson plan "What's Your Digital Platform?" for more ideas in the Appendix.

Technology presents barriers and opportunities for students with differing abilities. These students have additional risk factors that can make self-regulating and communicating harder. That means digital spaces are potentially less safe. Digital citizenship is important for all students, but particularly ones at high risk. Teaching inclusively to them can have long-ranging impact.

Chapter Wrap-Up

This chapter addressed inclusivity to the neurodiverse, those who learn and think differently. School leaders should provide support and help for educators to adapt to their learners. They should also be aware that technology has different effects on different brains.

Chapter 6 shifts the topic to community and partnership building. To make large-scale change, school leaders need to have difficult conversations with many stakeholders. The next chapter offers specific ideas on how to accomplish this, as well as how to effectively market and reach the entire school community.

CHAPTER 6

Learning from Community Partners and Policymakers

Digital citizenship affects us all. How can we bring together partners to expand the conversation? This chapter offers strategies for outreach and communications related to digital citizenship and includes examples of real-life trials and successes of expanding digital citizenship education to an entire state.

Digital citizenship exists not only in education but also in politics. The U.S. federal government, state legislatures, and local governments all discuss and pass bills and make decisions around technology, free speech, privacy, and more. This chapter will help the reader find common ground with those policy makers so that school leaders and elected officials can work together to expand digital citizenship in an inclusive and research-based way.

By the end of this chapter you will:

- get suggestions on how to have difficult conversations around the topic of digital citizenship
- understand some of the processes for scaling education programs
- understand how marketing, outreach, and community engagement can support digital citizenship initiatives

Navigating the Politics of Digital Citizenship

I (Carrie) never realized how political the topic of digital citizenship was until I was already in the thick of it. In 2019, my company received a five-year contract as the official online safety provider in the state of Utah. We received the contract after a monthslong procurement that culminated into a presentation to a committee. I was ecstatic when we won. We had been working in this space for years and had spent thousands of hours refining our curriculum, getting survey data, and creating connections and partnerships in the space. I, somewhat naively, thought that after this rigorous bidding process, it would be smooth sailing—data and government procurement had prevailed. But that was not the case.

As soon as we got the contract, the previous vendor began a political and public relations campaign. A survey from that vendor with disinformation and pre-filled-out responses was posted and shared online. I had to involve the attorney general's office to send a cease and desist letter. Misinformation was shared with schools and organizations about us. A lobbyist connected to the other vendor launched a behind-doors campaign. The lobbyist recruited principals to call and complain to educational staff about how we delivered our program. We offered classroom-based learning, not assemblies. This teaching approach was criticized by some of those principals, and then brought up at an information-gathering meeting organized by a legislator connected to that lobbyist with the implicit, if not explicit, intent to take our contract. At the same time I was working on scaling and marketing our program, I was also spending time talking, teaching, and reaching out to organizations and individuals to try to counter the confusion.

A main complaint of this other vendor then (and now) was that our program did not serve as many students. The other vendor had assemblies: short, energetic talks to the entire student body. There were no discussions or activities, nor any tracking of knowledge, behavior, or attitude changes over a period of time—but the talks definitely generated publicity. Our program was classroom-based, full of activities, and spread out over a longer period of time. On paper we reached fewer students, but we had significantly more classes and direct work with students. From our surveys, observations, and discussions with students, we found this made an impact on their knowledge, attitudes, and behavior toward digital citizenship.

An additional obstacle was changing the model. Although our contract mentioned online safety, we addressed safety through the holistic concept of digital citizenship. This meant multiple classes on different topics, all with the goal of building skills to help keep kids safe. It took longer to explain our program, and it certainly wasn't as flashy. The other program had also been running for over a decade—a long time in the world of education. Principals and teachers had gotten used to it; it was comfortable, safe, and easier to schedule than multiple classes.

Perhaps you have dealt with this before. You're trying something new but are meeting resistance. Explaining concepts like digital citizenship takes time; they aren't easily condensed into a slogan. Your colleagues, like you, are busy, and sometimes may gravitate toward the simplest—though not necessarily the best—solution for students. Maybe you're not having to deal with misinformation campaigns, lawyers, and lobbyists, but if you're trying to implement any kind of change on a large scale, you're going to have to deal with strong feelings. When someone tries to start something new, others may perceive it as a territorial threat: *"What was wrong with what I was doing before?"*

> The goal of digital citizenship is to develop empowered, educated, safe, and inclusive students. That's a big goal, with a focus on the quality of digital citizenship education, not the quantity of students you can fit into a gym for an assembly. To achieve such a goal, you need to spend as much time building relationships as you do building research and data to support the change.

I definitely dealt with strong emotions—and those emotions are publicly available on the Utah legislature's website (Utah State Legislature, 2021). There was a coordinated, but failed, campaign by a lobbyist to get my contract canceled. I had to testify and then listen to misinformation directly from the previous vendor—while I stayed silent in the audience. It was extremely stressful, but I believed then, as I do now, that when making change you have to keep in mind the bigger picture. The goal of digital citizenship is to develop empowered, educated, safe, and inclusive students. That's a big goal, with a focus on the quality of digital citizenship education, not the quantity of students you can fit into a gym for an assembly. To achieve such a goal, you need to spend as much time building relationships as you do building research and data to support the change.

BUILDING A DIGITAL CITIZENSHIP COALITION

Chapter 2 describes coalition building to make systemic change in L.A. Unified School District. They assembled various groups, both internal and external, to discuss digital citizenship policy and implement professional learning. The entire school community were potential parts of that coalition. The Visionary Planner indicator 3.2.d of the ISTE Standards for Education Leaders describes some of this coalition-building process in "communicate effectively with stakeholders to gather input on the plan, celebrate successes and engage in a continuous improvement cycle" (ISTE, 2018).

Other tips for building a digital citizenship coalition include:

- Determine definitions and goals first.
- Set up a mailing list/email group or communication repository for all the members. To keep engagement going send out emails regularly and have a place to share and store meeting minutes, goals, and future plans.
- Work to build personal relationships with coalition members. A moderator/organizer of a meeting should make sure to call on others. Thank your coalition members regularly and have individual check-ins if you don't see or hear from someone.
- Have regular meetings at the same time and place. If possible, set a meeting schedule for the entire school year. At every meeting, assign action items to members.

Digital citizenship is political—not just because of some of the topics covered but also the emotions involved. When it comes to technology and children, people have strong feelings. It can be a struggle to build those relationships when you feel attacked or to try to find common ground when it seems there is none. But digital citizenship should be active and outward. This means speaking up, sharing, and working to make social change. As indicated in Education Leader Standard 3.1.c, school leaders should be equity and citizenship advocates and "model digital citizenship" by "engaging in civil discourse," even when that is not easy to do (ISTE, 2018).

RELATED ISTE STANDARDS

This chapter focuses on conversations and coalition building. An important part of a school leader's role is to work with various stakeholders on common grounds. This work relates to the following ISTE Standards:

ISTE STANDARDS FOR EDUCATION LEADERS: 3.1 EQUITY AND CITIZENSHIP ADVOCATE

- 3.1.c Model digital citizenship by critically evaluating online resources, engaging in civil discourse online and using digital tools to contribute to positive social change.

ISTE STANDARDS FOR EDUCATION LEADERS: 3.2 VISIONARY PLANNER

- 3.2.d Communicate effectively with stakeholders to gather input on the plan, celebrate successes and engage in a continuous improvement cycle.
- 3.2.e Share lessons learned, best practices, challenges and the impact of learning with technology with other education leaders who want to learn from this work.

ISTE STANDARDS FOR EDUCATION LEADERS: 3.4 SYSTEMS DESIGNER

- 3.4.d Establish partnerships that support the strategic vision, achieve learning priorities and improve operations.

This chapter will build on topics discussed in Chapters 2 and 4 and go deeper into dealing with perceptions and building common ground. It will also share practical tips from experts with on-the-ground experiences of managing hard conversations and navigating social and governmental politics. If you want to scale and broaden digital citizenship across a community, conversations and relationship-building are both critical.

Strategies for Managing Difficult Conversations

Caitlin McDonald is the program manager for the Center for Local Initiatives at Utah Humanities. A big part of her job is organizing and facilitating community conversations—and many of those conversations are controversial. McDonald describes her experience in a "fishbowl conversation" about abortion.

> *I could tell walking in to the room that there was already tension in the air, I think partially because the topic itself divided us into two groups. The fishbowl method starts with one side starting out sitting in an inner circle, with the other side sitting in an outer circle. The outer circle must listen to the inner circle have a conversation about their own beliefs, then the groups switch.*
>
> *One of the women who was most fired up about the topic mentioned how valuable it was that she was forced to listen to the other side without speaking, because it gave her a chance to actually hear them without thinking about how she was going to defend her side. By the end, multiple people realized that they found common ground, such as better health care for women. It was a good lesson for me as a facilitator, particularly with a controversial topic. No one convinced the other side to change their beliefs, but everyone was put in a space where they better understood each other. (interview, October 2021)*

McDonald feels that having a conversation on these emotional topics with the goal of changing beliefs is misguided. People get defensive. They close down and they spend less time listening and more time preparing their response (interview, October 2021). McDonald says that "the best way to start a conversation is with curiosity rather than judgment. Never assume you know what the other person believes, or why they believe something" (interview, October 2021).

> When I teach digital parenting classes I always start off with an open-ended question: "What do you see?" This not only gives me a sense of what topics the parents want to cover for what ages, but gives them a chance to share their beliefs and values. The audience may not always agree with what I have to say, and vice versa, but at least there's open sharing of information, and I'm genuinely curious and interested in what they have to say.

When I teach digital parenting classes I always start off with an open-ended question: "What do you see?" This not only gives me a sense of what topics the parents want to cover for what ages, but gives them a chance to share their beliefs and values. The audience may not always agree with what I have to say, and vice versa, but at least there's open sharing of information, and I'm genuinely curious and interested in what they have to say. I let that first part of the class go on as long as it needs to, and give space for everyone to talk. I make sure to repeat and validate what they have to say. Scan the QR code for more insights into running a digital parenting event.

This practice of listening and then repeating what the other side has said is common in marriage and family therapy, but educators can also apply this strategy to hold difficult conversations. Dr. John Gottman is a marriage researcher who's spent 40 years observing thousands of couples. He developed a method for handling conflict based on Dr. Lydia Rapoport's work in crisis intervention. For the Gottman-Rapoport intervention to work, participants must agree on two main principles: 1) They must agree that there are "two valid realities" with a focus on perception, not facts, and 2) Everyone must feel "heard and understood." If both sides don't feel heard and understood, no change can be made, nor common ground be found (Gottman & Gottman, 2015).

TIPS FOR HOSTING A DIGITAL PARENTING EVENT

To apply this intervention in a facilitated conversation:

1. Both sides must understand and agree on the two core principles.
2. The facilitator explains the roles of the speaker and listener like so:
    a. Speaker:
        i. Only use "I" statements.
        ii. Do not place blame on the other party.
        iii. State a *positive* need.
    b. Listener
        i. Hear the speaker's needs and tone.
        ii. Summarize the speaker's needs and tone to the speaker's satisfaction.
        iii. Validate the speaker.
3. The speaker should hold the floor without interruption. They can be prompted by the facilitator. After the speaker finishes, and the listener summarizes and validates, the roles are reversed (Gottman & Gottman, 2015).

ESTABLISHING CLEAR, ACHIEVABLE GOALS

If you are working within the school, district, or even the state level, the financial component of a new project or program is just the first step. Just because there's money for digital citizenship doesn't mean a robust digital citizenship program will be implemented. There are logistics to keep in mind and many, many more conversations to be had. But before those conversations start, it's helpful to do a gut check, to take a step back and ask: What are my goals? Are they realistic, achievable, and in line with my partner's mindset on digital citizenship?

Is my goal to . . .

. . . educate the person about what digital citizenship is?

. . . correct the person about what digital citizenship is?

. . . get this person to practice digital citizenship?

. . . change their attitudes around digital citizenship?

. . . know about their experiences with digital citizenship?

. . . understand their perception of digital citizenship?

Other community members may have different, sometimes conflicting, goals. The Prosci ADKAR Model for change management described in Chapter 1 describes five elements that are needed for successful change, beginning with the "awareness of the need to change" (Hiatt, 2006). This is something to address in those initial, sometimes difficult, conversations. Understand that your goals might not be realistic, or they may not be perceived as urgent or necessary.

For initial conversations, consider centering your goals around the other person rather than yourself: to know and understand their experiences and perceptions of digital citizenship. Behavioral change happens slowly, and systemic change often even slower. Trust has to be built first.

From "Now What?" to "What Do You Think?"

McDonald has hosted many facilitated conversations, and afterwards, she sometimes gets the question, "So now what?" She says:

> There are always those who feel like a conversation is perhaps a waste of time, because it doesn't accomplish anything tangible. The reality is that the conversation is an accomplishment, because it is the first step in taking productive action. Without understanding, so much of our interactions are completely unproductive—we will continue to shout in an echo chamber without being able to create solutions that serve a spectrum of different beliefs. (interview, October 2021)

The "Now what?" question comes from Bolman and Deal's Four-Frame Model; specifically, the Structural frame (Bolman & Deal, 2021). As discussed in Chapter 1, this frame relates to task management and involves creating metrics and setting deadlines. Administrators likely see much of their role through this frame. But one cannot create those tasks without a shared mission and value set. In these early conversations, which are needed to create larger-scale change, an administrator should temper their desire to ask "What next?" and instead ask "What do you think?"

> Finding the pain point is the first step in persuasion, and eventually to a sale. But outside the sales world, this way of looking at conversations and relationship can help build common ground.

What Is the Pain Point?

Another way to frame the open-ended question "What do you think?" is to determine the "pain points" of what that person and/or their organization is experiencing. This is a term used in business and sales to describe a persistent problem with a product or service that annoys customers. Finding the pain point is the first step in persuasion, and eventually to a sale. But outside the sales world, this way of looking at conversations and relationship can help build common ground.

What are the pain points that are stopping or slowing down your digital citizenship goals? In my experience, I've found the pain points rather quickly. Providing educational services can be like providing services in a restaurant or retail store. Customers—or in the case of schools, parents or students—are more likely to complain about a service than praise it. A strong negative emotion, or that pain point, is more likely to drive someone to write a negative review or send an email than a calming, positive emotion. When implementing digital citizenship on a large scale, the feedback we got from teachers and administrators on their pain points included:

- **What?** What is digital citizenship? What is the need for this?
- **Why?** Why the change from assemblies to classroom learning? Why are we using this model to teach digital citizenship? Why not just teach online safety?
- **How?** How do I book a class? Who do I need to talk to? What are the classes about? How long are the classes? What supplies are needed?
- **When?** How can I find the time to schedule and communicate about this? How can I fit this into the school day?

The logistics (How?) and time (When?) pain points were relatively easy to deal with. We created infographics to explain how to book the program. We had a dedicated number and email to contact. We added multiple contact forms on our website and got partner organizations and districts to advertise the program. We spent time on the phone and email explaining the program and worked around schools' schedules. It still continues to take a lot of time and conversations to schedule. While we can streamline things with technology and logistical processes, scheduling is also about relationship building; it provides an opportunity to explain what digital citizenship is and why it's important.

> Customers—or in the case of schools, parents or students—are more likely to complain about a service than praise it. A strong negative emotion, or that pain point, is more likely to drive someone to write a negative review or send an email than a calming, positive emotion.

The "What?" and "Why?" pain points are more time consuming. As noted, they involve relationship building, conversations, dealing with strong emotions, and sometimes multiple calls and emails. You will never fully answer everyone's "What?" and "Why?" questions, but that's OK. You will never get everyone fully up

> ## THE ROLE OF PARENTS AND CAREGIVERS
>
> Parents and caregivers are vital members of the school community. They're also integral when it comes to implementing digital citizenship. Research shows that how parents use technology predicts how children use technology (Starks, 2021). Parents can reinforce any digital citizenship learning done at home.
>
> Parents and caregivers have (legitimate) fears or pain points when it comes to technology. A 2020 Pew Research survey found that two-thirds of parents in the United States feel "parenting is harder today than it was 20 years ago" and many cited technology as the reason why (Auxier, et al., 2020).
>
> School leaders can help defuse parent and caregiver pain points by sharing the positives of educational technology. ISTE Standard for Education Leaders 3.2: Visionary Planner encourages school leaders to "share lessons learned, best practices, challenges and the impact of learning with technology" (ISTE, 2018). These lessons should not just be shared with colleagues, but parents as well. Parents may only hear about the negatives through school alerts, the media, and so on, so school leaders should make sure to share the positives.

to speed and dedicated to the practice—it's not realistic to expect 100% compliance and enthusiastic motivation. People are motivated by different things, and sometimes there's no way to fully overcome pain points. But it's important to keep trying anyway. It shows you care and are dedicated; and you try again because sometimes you just might have caught someone on a bad day.

Even in our politically polarized environment, common ground can be found. An example of this is the increase of bills from both Republicans and Democrats in the U.S. Congress in 2021 aimed at reigning in social media companies. Both political parties were concerned about speech and content moderation online. Members of both parties grilled tech CEOs and others in Congressional Hearings. However, there were differences in their perceptions and value around speech. Democrats, through proposed bills like the PACT Act, would make it easier to take down user speech. Republicans in Florida and Texas passed laws (now challenged in court) in their legislatures about social media companies' ability to moderate content based on viewpoint and politics (Mullin, 2021). While some of the concerns around speech are different, both parties have a similar pain point: distrust and discomfort with the power of social media platforms.

The best way to find a pain point is to simply ask. All of us have our issues regarding technology. Starting off with curiosity with school community partners will bring out those pain points. Sometimes school leaders feel they know the issues and they begin conversations by telling the audience the issues. It should be the other way around.

Scaling Digital Citizenship

Rick Gainsford has been involved in the digital citizenship world since the early 1990s. Currently the education technology specialist with the Utah State Board of Education (USBE), Gainsford remembers what it was like decades ago talking about technology at the state level. In the beginnings of the internet, most all of the resources USBE had were gopher sites "housed at universities. So there was a fair amount of safety built into the system." But that quickly changed (interview, August 2021). He explains:

> It was one of the first meetings I had at the state, we sat down with several senators and representatives and leadership at Utah Education Network (UEN) because they were concerned, and rightly so. You had two avenues of thought at that time—first was we could deploy filtering solutions that will block the vast majority of inappropriate material. Second we create a white list of resources, we only allow students to visit certain sources. It was easy when there were only 1,000 websites! (interview, August 2021)

Filtering and blocking is *much* easier with only 1,000 websites, but those 1,000 websites multiplied quickly. The Utah State Board of Education and other state leaders realized they needed another solution; there was no way to filter through everything while ensuring students still had the access they needed. Gainsford says they developed (and continue to use) the following three tactics:

- filtering
- creating and sharing acceptable use policies that both students and parents understand and sign
- a shared understanding that the best filter is "essentially the mind of every user—and so it's critical to teach good judgment and encourage users to reach out to a trusted adult if they encounter anything questionable/problematic" (interview, August 2021).

Everyone Has a Stake in the Topic

Policies and approaches to education must change with the times. The internet of 1992 is long gone—so is the internet of 2002 and, for that matter, 2012. Filters and acceptable use/device policies are still part of digital citizenship, but current approaches must include more. Education on digital citizenship is needed, and as Gainsford suggests, collaboration is more important than before because technology affects everyone, not just technology professionals. "I think that what we try to do at the state level is that everyone has a stake in this," he says. "This is not the purview of just the tech people; it's the village coming together" (interview, August 2021).

McDonald shares Gainford's sentiment, saying, "In organizations, particularly those that serve the public, when creating policy the most important thing is to involve the communities and stakeholders with whom they work. The *worst* thing to do when developing new policies is to do so without the input of those who are affected by them" (interview, October 2021). And, like discussed in Chapter 4, some of those stakeholders whose voices are most needed encounter barriers to access and participation.

> "In organizations, particularly those that serve the public, when creating policy the most important thing is to involve the communities and stakeholders with whom they work. The *worst* thing to do when developing new policies to do so without the input of those who are affected by them" (interview, October 2021).

Gainsford describes some of the stakeholders he's collaborated with in creating state guidelines and policies.

> We work with the tech people to build in those tech solutions. We have to bring administrators and leaders in buildings and provide the tools and resources and understanding of what to do...You have to bring in your parents, both through acceptable use, but it's not just signing that form, they have a responsibility in that as well. (interview, August 2021)

All stakeholders have different perceptions and may not be aware of problems experienced by others. For example, a teacher may see some educational videos on YouTube they want their students to watch as homework. But a parent may be concerned about content on YouTube, or not have the broadband speed or access to a device to watch those videos.

Some of those concerns can be brought to light through:

- **Needs assessment.** These can help answer the "what"—as in, "what is happening in my community?" (See the Appendix and the book's companion site for some specific ideas of things to include in a needs assessment.)
- **Gap analysis.** An investigation can identify the "how" for the questions in the needs assessment, indicating who is responsible for tasks and prioritizing them.
- **Community conversations.** Conversations outside the school building help school leaders have a better understanding of the pain points and values of the school community.
- **Focus groups.** These smaller, intimate groups help expand on topics and pain points brought up in community conversations. They provide more context to the content shared through surveys and conversations.
- **Open forums with a knowledgeable facilitator.** Open forums are both a space for gathering and sharing information. They can be used to collect community feedback on topics as well as disseminate goals and future plans.
- **Community surveys.** These are a bird's-eye level glimpse into a community's beliefs and values.

COMPANION SITE

Politicians draft and advocate for laws. School administrators create policies. Teachers craft lesson plans and educate. Parents mentor and model tech behavior. We all have a responsibility to promote and advocate for digital citizenship.

Marketing, Outreach, and Engagement

As discussed in Chapters 1 and 4, there are different definitions and ideas about digital citizenship. Some may view digital citizenship through an online safety lens; others may have a different definition altogether. And before any marketing, outreach, or engagement happens, school communities should try to get on the same page. School leaders should use the same definitions and reference the same standards, whether it be from ISTE or the state. If there's inconsistent branding, different verbiage, or different responses to the same topic, it causes confusion and can set back the school's goals. Once there's general agreement on a definition, then it's time to take next steps.

Perhaps you're creating an open forum for community input or putting on a digital parenting event, or maybe you want to share some results from a digital citizenship program in your district. How do you get the word out? Just because something is free for the community doesn't mean people will come. And just because digital citizenship is an important topic doesn't mean everyone agrees on what it is, or what to do about it, or even *want* to share their thoughts. This means school leadership must engage in marketing, outreach, and community engagement. Table 6.1 outlines some of the different methods you can use.

TABLE 6.1 Ideas for Marketing, Outreach, and Engagement

	MARKETING	OUTREACH	ENGAGEMENT
What is it?	Functions in identifying and persuading an audience	Short-term style of marketing done to reach a larger audience not typically served through traditional marketing techniques	A long-term process of creating relationships with stakeholders
Goals	Get people to complete a specific activity and to have awareness of a product/service	Help define the audience to reach, share information, gather, information, and seek buy-in/approval of programs/projects	Provide space for the community to collaborate, share concerns, and be empowered to act in their own interests
Examples	Newsletter Social media Emails	Tabling a booth Holding a focus group	One-on-one meetings Serving on a council/board

One way to look at the difference between outreach, marketing, and engagement is that outreach and marketing are done *for* or *to* the audience, whereas community engagement is done *with* the audience. Outreach and marketing are more transactional, with a specific purpose, whereas community engagement is long-term and foundational (Building the Field of Community Engagement, 2014).

When scaling digital citizenship, long-term community engagement should be the ultimate goal. However, short-term objectives are best reached through marketing or community outreach. All three methods must be used to create sustainable and cohesive change.

When thinking through what method to use, ask yourself these questions:

- Do I want to reach a new or broader audience?
    - *Marketing* is best for your existing audience; these are the people already on your email list and in your community. *Outreach* is the best method for reaching other members of the community.
- Do I want to advertise my event?
    - For any advertising—whether for an event, a resource, to share positive stories, etc.—*marketing* is the method to use. For ideas of marketing emails, see the Appendix.
- Do I want the community to plan their own events?
    - Community *engagement* is a long-term process of empowering other stakeholders. It's a way to identify and support champions of your school's work and ideas (Building the Field of Community Engagement, 2014).

In my work, I ask all of my staff to contribute a few hours a week of outreach and community engagement. All staff are required to join a community group. Over the years they've served on nonprofit boards and school community councils, been part of parent groups, or participated with professional associations. On average staff attend 20-plus outreach events or meetings a month around the state. This can definitely be time-consuming and costly, but it's paid off in terms of the relationships we've built. Outreach is a stepping stone to engagement that can take you on the path to implementation and the long-term destination of changing digital citizenship culture.

Scaling digital citizenship is about shifting a culture, a perception. It's understandable that communities want bigger attendance at events and greater participation in the process—getting a big crowd at an event or lots of shares from a blog post feels good. Ultimately, however, the biggest goal is creating an empowered community.

This community writes their own blog posts and puts on their own events. They are passionate and proactive. The students in this empowered community make their own decisions to be positive online without being reminded by parents and teachers. Think bigger. Expand our goals beyond numbers and crowds and instead focus on changing the culture. Aim for more than a school community educated in digital citizenship. You want them *empowered* in digital citizenship.

That's a lofty and ambitious goal, I know. Implementation and change are hard, involve many stakeholders, and require a lot of time and energy. But a cultural shift in digital citizenship is a goal to keep in mind, to put on a Post-it somewhere and glance at once in a while. It may be ambitious, but it's achievable.

Working with Elected Officials

Representative Jon Hawkins is a member of the Utah House of Representatives. He was elected in 2019 in District 57 and is the co-chair of the Digital Citizenship and Wellness Commission. His full-time job is in the tech industry, and he works with education, business, and other leaders in the state (Utah State Legislature, 2022). In his role as a legislator, he talks frequently with those who disagree with him. Hawkins follows the proverb that "you win more friends with honey than vinegar" (interview, January 2022). He shares a story of how he worked to find a common goal.

> A couple of years ago I ran a vaping bill that . . . raised the legal smoking age to 21 to meet the national requirement and then it put vaping products inside of specialty shops. The goal was to curb youth vaping. But there's some things about the bill that not everybody liked, but they were united around that goal: "We want to make sure kids aren't delving into vaping products when they shouldn't be." . . . Even though we were on different sides of the proverbial aisle the goal to ensure kids safety and health with vaping products was the ultimate goal. When you can rally around a common goal I think it helps bridge any common divides. (interview, January 2022)

While people may have different perspectives on technology and the practice of digital citizenship, they can still share common goals.

While people may have different perspectives on technology and the practice of digital citizenship, they can still share common goals. Hawkins recommends the common goal to "teach general practices like proper use of time, proper use of technology, what situations might become dangerous, and who to trust and who not to trust on technology" (interview, January 2022).

In Chapter 4, we examined the different perceptions of digital citizenship from various school community members. Let's add to that table to include the different perceptions of elected officials. To be clear, individuals can work across multiple frames (as mentioned in Chapter 4, principals can also view things through the Symbolic frame, for example). Table 6.2 summarizes which framework is most common based on the responsibilities of the job.

TABLE 6.2 Frames Most Commonly Associated with Key Roles

	PRINCIPALS	PARENTS	TEACHERS	ELECTED OFFICIALS
Frame	Structural	Symbolic	Symbolic	Political
Focus	Behavior/staffing	Feeling purpose and a desire for control	Curriculum, standards, and outcomes	Coalition and power base building

Elected officials are the ones who know the decision-makers, who work with interest groups, build coalitions and may know about hidden agendas the public is not aware of. They have to make difficult choices with limited budgets and pressure from many sides (Bolman & Deal, 2021).

Coalition-Building and Finding Common Ground

As Table 6.2 shows, to find common ground, one should find a goal that can inspire and motivate people, has a clear plan and strategy, and has enough political support behind it—using the Symbolic, Structural, and Political frames, respectively (Bolman & Deal, 2021). A great slogan that gets people excited won't have enough movement and support if there isn't an actionable plan for making progress. A popular idea with just parents or just teachers won't move forward unless there's a broader coalition behind it.

Rep. Hawkins also explains the importance of building a coalition when it comes to working with state legislators.

> *One of the things that people don't understand is that I'm only one vote. You need at least 38 votes to get bills passed in the House, and then the Senate and then the Governor. And it's even worse if you don't want the governor involved because you need to get 2/3 to pass it through. People tend to put blame on individual representatives, but I'm only just one vote. (interview, January 2022)*

Being able to pass a bigger education budget or start a new state program requires working with different organizations and interests. You have to have enough votes. Hawkins also sees misconceptions around the role of state versus federal elected officials. "I don't really interact with Congress that much. I try to interact with county and local governments. Congress is hard because there's 435 representatives, 100 Senators—so it's even more difficult" (interview, January 2022).

Education comes from local, state, and federal funding. Understanding where the pockets of money are located and who has control over that funding is important for school leaders to implement and spread digital citizenship learning for their schools.

School Leaders as Thought Leaders

School leaders have an opportunity to be thought leaders to elected officials. This is part of the ISTE Education Leader Standard 3.4: Systems Designer, which states that school leaders should "establish partnerships that support the strategic vision" (ISTE, 2018). School leaders can be subject experts, advise on councils, share information, keep in touch, and more. "First off, I'm not the expert on everything," Hawkins says. "People expect me to be the expert on everything. What I tend to do is lean on others who have expertise or a lot of knowledge in that area and try to point people in the right direction" (interview, January 2022).

School leaders can make their expertise and knowledge easier to find and access, which can make it easier for data to be disseminated and understood. To facilitate this, consider creating a repository of digital citizenship resources. When reporting statistics, use easy-to-follow graphs and summarize the data. Share stories from the district that back up the data. Make sure people know about the repository. Market it, and go to outreach events. Hawkins says to know your legislator, but not approach them saying, "You're an idiot, you have to do this." Instead, try, "Hey, here's an idea. How can we help make this happen?" (interview, January 2022).

To summarize, here are strategies for school leaders who want to work with elected officials to scale a digital citizenship solution:

- Remember that elected officials are typically operating under the political framework of the Four-Frame Model. They come at different issues through a lens of knowing what is popular, who has the power, and who would need to be involved to make something happen. This often means compromising a vision and having difficult conversations.
- Know where the money comes from. Is it at a state level? Federal? Somewhere else?
- Find a common goal that can satisfy different school community groups.
- Become a knowledge expert. Create a repository of research-based and vetted information on digital citizenship, and share it with elected officials.

Chapter Wrap-Up

I wish I knew back when my company got our state's contract what I know now, a few years into scaling digital citizenship. It's a much more political process than I thought; good intentions and ideas only go so far. To succeed, you need a strategy, a coalition behind you, and the ability to work with many people who may not only disagree with you, but may also want to see you removed.

This chapter covered conversations, coalitions, and confrontations. To create and implement change takes an entire community and good listening skills. In Chapter 7, we'll dive deeper into implementation, and also share practices for making things happen and how to use educational standards to support educators.

CHAPTER 7

Implementing Digital Citizenship and the ISTE Standards

The final chapter of this book shares ideas and strategies for implementing digital citizenship practice on a large scale. Digital citizenship is found throughout the ISTE Standards; in particular, the Standards for Students, Educators, and Education Leaders help scale and standardize the practice. This chapter also discusses inclusive teaching across multiple grade levels and offers suggestions on what to focus on at different ages. Tips on planning and incorporating digital citizenship into school culture and the classroom are also included.

By the end of this chapter you will:

- recognize how to use the ISTE Standards to scale digital citizenship
- know more about the process of implementing education policy and programs
- understand how to teach digital citizenship at different grade levels

Classroom Tools for Moving Your Program Forward

Teaching a class of educators is like teaching digital citizenship to a classroom of students. Both groups include participants with different abilities, backgrounds, and experiences. Both will have eager learners as well as some who are less enthusiastic; you may hear groans from both students and educators, with students wondering, "Why do I need this? It's not part of my class!" and educators asking, "Why do I need this? It's not part of my job."

Digital citizenship is relevant to many education roles, and it is included in the ISTE Standards for Educators; Standard 2.3 Citizen includes four unique indicators related to the topic. For example, indicator 2.3.a asks educators to "create experiences for learners to make positive, socially responsible contributions and exhibit empathetic behavior online that builds relationships and community" (ISTE, 2017).

I (Carrie) remember teaching a class of teachers from a secondary school, which included a range of educators—mathematics and English teachers, a media specialist, an administrator, and so on. It was a great class, but it did remind me of teaching students. Like with a class of children, there were a few educators who had arrived early and were talkative, actively participating. And there was one in the back with their head down, on the phone. The irony of talking about digital wellness topics while someone was buried in a phone did not escape me.

This book is dedicated to helping education leaders implement and manage change. Like we've said earlier: change is hard. It's difficult to get buy-in and make things happen. But change is possible, even in near-immovable systems and with educators who don't want to participate. This chapter provides more tools for educators and school leaders to make the changes needed to build a robust digital citizenship program from the ground up. We'll walk through a number of tools that can help you in the process, including standards and frameworks, and curriculum and planning support.

Practice can be harder than policymaking. You can create a policy in one day, but you have to practice it for years. This chapter gives specific recommendations from experts, policy-makers, and practitioners to turn best practices to best policies.

RELATED ISTE STANDARDS

The final chapter takes the foundation of policy and puts it into practice, focusing on conversations and coalition building. An important part of a school leader's role is to work with various stakeholders on common grounds, which relates to the following ISTE Standards:

ISTE STANDARDS FOR EDUCATORS: 2.2 LEADER

- 2.2.b Advocate for equitable access to educational technology, digital content and learning opportunities to meet the diverse needs of all students.

ISTE STANDARDS FOR EDUCATORS: 2.3 CITIZEN

- 2.3.a Create experiences for learners to make positive, socially responsible contributions and exhibit empathetic behavior online that build relationships and community.

ISTE STANDARDS FOR EDUCATION LEADERS: 3.5 CONNECTED LEARNER

- 3.5.d Develop the skills needed to lead and navigate change, advance systems and promote a mindset of continuous improvement for how technology can improve learning.

ISTE STANDARDS FOR STUDENTS: 1.1 EMPOWERED LEARNER

- 1.1.a. Students articulate and set personal learning goals, develop strategies leveraging technology to achieve them and reflect on the learning process itself to improve learning outcomes.

ISTE STANDARDS FOR STUDENTS: 1.2 DIGITAL CITIZEN

- 1.2.b Students engage in positive, safe, legal and ethical behavior when using technology, including social interactions online or when using networked devices.
- 1.2.c Students demonstrate an understanding of and respect for the rights and obligations of using and sharing intellectual property.

Strategies for Implementation

Claus von Zastrow is the senior director of policy with the Education Commission of the States (ECS), a nonpartisan organization that monitors education policy and provides advice to policymakers across the United States. He oversees initiatives in education policy, conducts research, helps states find information on key education issues, and partners with other policy organizations. His team works closely with other directors to help guide policy and make sure that ECS is responsive to state leaders. ECS does not advocate for specific policies, but collaborates with hundreds of education commissioners that work with policymakers throughout the country to inform them about other organizations' work on education issues, policy options and more (interview, December 2021).

For school leaders trying to implement education policy or a new program, such as a digital citizenship initiative, von Zastrow offers: "One of the things that a school leader has to think about first and foremost is where are state leaders able to have an impact. What's the role of a state leader as opposed to a local leader?" As mentioned in Chapter 6, there are federal, state, and local controls, and school leaders may not be able to have as much impact in some of those areas. von Zastrow continues, "Very often the role of a state leader is to create the conditions for it to happen, rather than require it to happen" (interview, December 2021).

How can school leaders create the conditions for adoption and implementation? Here are some recommendations based on von Zastrow's insights:

- **Provide incentives.** Incentives help create the environment for adoption and change. "Those incentives can include funding," von Zastrow explains. "An example would be states saying, 'We have some means of vetting digital literacy curriculum for effectiveness.' And they could say, 'Well, if that's the case we will give funding for districts who apply to put these projects in place.' In that way they're creating an incentive, districts can see the value of this—then the state leaders can help create some more direction" (interview, December 2021). Providing incentives is a different approach to making mandates. An incentive is more of a soft push: a carrot, rather than a stick. School leaders can make their own determinations on which approach is best, but if there is some kind of mandate (a "stick"), they should make absolutely certain they are staying in their role and following policies and laws.

- **Build trust.** Educators and staff should have trust in their administration and that the adoption of new programs is transparent and research-based. "I do think trust is a challenge," von Zastrow says. "Part of it is wondering, 'Why this particular program?' and "Who's benefitting?' So third-party reviewers are always a good deal" (interview, December 2021).

- **Provide resources and support.** Administrators should provide support, whether that be training, time, or additional funding to make sure programs are implemented well. "As with anything else in education reform, good ideas badly implemented can kill the idea and set it way way back," says von Zastrow. "Things can be badly implemented if they don't have the resources, or they don't have the leadership support . . . if there isn't really good training." von Zastrow worked in STEM policy before his current role and recognized the importance of support then as well, relating, "I've seen it in less sensitive areas like new science curricula . . . if teachers aren't really given the time or support they need to implement good curriculum, then the data suggests that the curriculum doesn't really happen, or it happens in ways that the designer didn't intend. Then teachers say it wasn't effective and they'll say it was stressful and they didn't know it—and they'll be right. Then a great program will end up on the dust heap for a while" (interview, December 2021).

> Administrators should provide support, whether that be training, time, or additional funding to make sure programs are implemented well.

- **Use standards when implementing new programs.** If states and districts are using agreed-upon standards, that can also help build trust in implementation. "Having an external source can be helpful for states so the states aren't saying, 'We're not doing this because we're politically connected to this person or program,'" says von Zastrow (interview, December 2021). This can be like using a third-party reviewer, so the process is not political.

- **Provide guidance and support on laws.** There are different state and federal laws around technology, like with the Children's Online Privacy Protection Act (COPPA) or ones around monitoring and data collection. "If you're an agency trying to address real-time challenges of digital behavior . . . you need to have the legal framework in place," recommends von Zastrow. Small districts may need additional supports to follow these laws and be in compliance. Claus von Zastrow gives the example of Louisiana, "which has one of the most stringent student data privacy laws in the country. One of the things the state education agency provides is guidance on what that means in complying with that law" (interview, December 2021).

These recommendations for administrators and school leaders are viewed through the Structural frame. Their jobs are to follow laws, create policies, and make them happen. But that framework can push against teachers and other staff. Part of this conflict is because of the administrator's role and perception. When something goes wrong, they're the ones to deal with it. Schools are blamed for not doing enough when a student is in crisis. Schools can also be sued when not following the laws.

Table 7.1 illustrates another conflict: perceiving digital citizenship as focusing only on online safety versus a concept to encourage online learning. The table lists contrasting values associated with each of the two topics. This is another area where teachers and administrators may be on different sides of the aisle.

TABLE 7.1 Digital Citizenship Values Through the Structural Frame: Online Safety vs. Online Learning

	ONLINE SAFETY	ONLINE LEARNING
STRUCTURAL FRAME VALUES AND IMPLEMENTATION	Creating policies	Reevaluating policies
	Using filters, restricting access	Allowing access
	Limiting screen time	Treating screen time as an opportunity for learning
	Saying "no" more than "yes"	Saying "yes" more than "no"

When school leaders are working to make change, they should preemptively create a process for making new policies and guidelines. Policies and laws should be less of a reaction to crises or media attention and more of a preventative tool to mitigate or altogether stop those crises from ever happening. But often new digital citizenship programs come as a result of a media scare or cyberbullying incident. If new programs and policies are implemented in a crisis, they may move so fast that not all voices are heard and the process is not transparent. Indicator 3.5.d of the Standards for Education Leaders addresses this change, stating that school leaders must "develop the skills needed to lead and navigate change" (ISTE, 2018). Some of those skills of change are discussed in Chapter 6, such as active listening, negotiating, and communicating. This communication and listening takes time.

When new change and policies are implemented quickly with a lack of communication, staff on the ground can lose trust and implementation may fail. Using the Structural frame, leaders may view digital citizenship more through an online safety lens than an online learning one, more concerned about laws, policies, and potential negative media attention. If school leaders look beyond the Structural frame of implementation to the Human Resources or Symbolic frame, they'll better understand how the program should be implemented. As discussed in Chapter 1, the Human Resources and Symbolic frames consider all stakeholders and emphasize the individuals in the system. By looking internally at people rather than externally at headlines, school leaders can keep the focus on digital citizenship where it should be—not only on safety but on students.

> When school leaders are working to make change, they should preemptively create a process for making new policies and guidelines. Policies and laws should be less of a reaction to crises or media attention and more of a preventative tool to mitigate or altogether stop those crises from ever happening.

Classroom teachers can also implement changes from the bottom to the top. But there are barriers, as Claus von Zastrow acknowledges. And teachers may know those barriers more than any other school leader. He advises as a first step that teachers "might turn to organizations like ISTE. They can look at these organizational structures and see if they can connect to the people there who are doing some of this work" (interview, December 2021). This can give teachers more perspective to know what's happening, and with whom to talk to make things happen in their area. There is also the potential ability for teachers to drive new programs and products. Each district and state has their own procurement process, which is how they vet those new programs. Sometimes the need for something new can start at the bottom, go to the principal, and then up the chain to district leaders who can then set that procurement process in motion.

> By looking internally at people rather than externally at headlines, school leaders can keep the focus on digital citizenship where it should be—not only on safety but on students.

Standards and Frameworks for Digital Citizenship Education

How do we teach digital citizenship? How do we teach such a multidisciplinary topic with disagreements on definitions, differing perceptions and priorities, and multiple school roles involved? As discussed in Chapter 3, the answer lies in creating a foundation for practice and professional learning with standards, guidelines, and frameworks. School leaders can help build something new, a framework that can support different school roles and ways of looking for things. Much like constructing a house, by building the foundation and the framework first, other educators can then add on, creating different "rooms" and collaborating on the design, all to construct a sturdy and long-lasting structure.

Rick Gainsford, who helped create the structure of digital teaching and learning in Utah in the early 1990s, describes his experience:

> We relied on trusted resources over the years; the ISTE standards always address internet safety and effective technology. We've built around them and adopted them. But as we put together our teaching and learning plan, we built around a framework that involved everyone: the superintendent, the students in the classroom, the teachers, the counselors, the parents at home, and the community members. They all need to have a better understanding of how we're trying to use technology in a way to promote better education. (interview, August 2021)

State and National Standards for Digital Citizenship

In addition to ISTE Standards, states and districts may have their own sets of standards around digital citizenship. They may also have different focuses and definitions. When scaling out new standards, it can be helpful for school leaders to compare and contrast those new standards with existing and more familiar ones.

For example, Tables 7.2a and 7.2b compare the New York State Education Department's (NYSED) new Computer Science and Digital Fluency Learning Standards on digital citizenship topics to ISTE's approach as seen in the ISTE Standards for Students and the DigCitCommit initiative (NYSED, 2021; ISTE, 2020). (Scan the QR code to learn more about DigCitCommit.)

DIGCITCOMMIT

TABLE 7.2A Similarities Between NYSED and ISTE Standards

NYSED	ISTE
Digital footprint: "Persistence of date on the internet"	Digital footprint: "Permanence of their actions in the digital world"
Internet for good: "Describe safe, appropriate, positive and responsible online behavior and identify strategies to combat negative behavior online."	Internet for good: "I use technology and digital channels for civic engagement, to solve problems and be a force for good…"
Safety (under Safeguards standard): "Describe common safeguards for protecting personal information."	Safety: "Students manage their personal data to maintain digital privacy and security…"

TABLE 7.2B Differences Between NYSED and ISTE Standards

NYSED	ISTE
Standards/outcomes on understanding intellectual property not included	"Students demonstrate an understanding of and respect for the rights and obligations of using and sharing intellectual property."
Some of the privacy/security standards are not listed under digital citizenship.	Privacy/security concerns under digital citizenship
Overall, more specific standards	Broader standards

State standards are more specific and detailed than ISTE Standards. They also are more targeted toward grade levels and specific coursework. Additionally, every state or organization's standards emphasize varying concepts of digital citizenship.

For example, compare the NYSED Computer Science and Digital Fluency Standards to ISTE's Student Standards and the five competencies in DigCitCommit. Both organizations include the digital footprint as part of digital citizenship and emphasize using technology for good in their student digital citizenship standards. On the other hand, ISTE includes intellectual property, a concept of digital law, in their standards, whereas NYSED does not. In addition, privacy and security standards are included in the ISTE Standards, but these are not listed under digital citizenship with NYSED.

Another way of looking at standards is using the visual model of the National School Library Standards developed by the American Association of School Librarians (AASL). These "crosswalks" compare multiple standards such as the Next Generation Science Standards and the ISTE Standards for Students and Educators via colorful documents. (AASL, 2021). Scan the QR code to view the crosswalks and examine the digital citizenship connections among the various sets of standards.

NATIONAL SCHOOL LIBRARY STANDARDS

There are similarities and differences in the ways that AASL and ISTE address digital citizenship in this crosswalk. For example, both AASL and ISTE encourage students to be global collaborators. AASL states in their Shared Foundations III. Collaborate, C. Share that "learners work productively with others to solve problems by: 1. Soliciting and responding to feedback from others. 2. Involving diverse perspectives in their own inquiry processes" (AASL, 2021). Both AASL and ISTE use student-centered language in their standards and encourage curiosity and the seeking of information. But AASL touches upon digital citizenship differently, from more of a media literacy angle. While ISTE's Standards for Students: Digital Citizen 1.2.c says students will "demonstrate an understanding of and respect for the rights and obligations of using and sharing intellectual property," AASL goes into more detail about that sharing and responsible use. This difference is because of the focus of the organizations. School librarians have more responsibilities around media literacy in their work than most other educators. They are typically the ones who manage or support computer labs and other types of technology, which makes responsible or acceptable use policies particularly relevant to their work.

Digital Citizenship and the ISTE Standards for Students

ISTE has a holistic approach to digital citizenship, covering various topics and addressing multiple audiences. Elements of digital citizenship can be found throughout the ISTE Standards for Students—for example, under the Computational Thinker, Global Collaborator, and Creative Communicator roles (ISTE, 2016).

Most predominately in the Student section, the Digital Citizen standard states that for students to be digital citizens, they must "recognize the rights, responsibilities and opportunities of living, learning and working in an interconnected digital world and . . . act and model in ways that are safe, legal and ethical" (ISTE, 2016). Drilling deeper, the standard includes four different indicators or learning outcomes to help educators better understand how to implement those standards. Those indicators touch on different elements of digital citizenship like digital footprint and digital identities in 1.2.a: "Students cultivate and manage their digital identity and reputation and are aware of the permanence of their actions in the digital world." The digital citizenship elements of online safety are found in the indicator 1.2.b: "Students engage in positive, safe, legal and ethical behavior when using technology, including social interactions online or when using networked devices" (ISTE, 2016). These indicators can help define and refine digital citizenship teaching in the classroom.

Carolyn Sykora, senior director of ISTE Standards Programs, helps create, disseminate, and evaluate those digital citizenship standards. But she does find gaps in the implementation around digital citizenship. "There's a lot of schools who do a good job, but they do it really intermittently . . . Doing it once or twice a year doesn't build that practice," she says. "I think there are ways to integrate; the standards are all about integration. There are ways to naturally integrate digital citizenship in courses" (interview, September 2021).

Part of this gap in integration comes from a lack of direction and support of teachers. In 2021, Sykora conducted a study with Helen Crompton, an associate professor of educational technology at Old Dominion University, evaluating instructional technology standards for educators. Published in the journal *Computers & Education*, the study found that educators struggled with transferring their technology knowledge from their personal and social lives into a classroom context (Crompton & Sykora, 2021). To help with this transfer of knowledge, they recommend that "the standards provide clear direction" with a "set of concrete examples" that would go along with each standard (Compton & Sykora, 2021).

But as mentioned earlier by von Zastrow, simply giving mandates and instructions is not enough. School leaders must provide incentives for adopting and implementing the standards. Crompton and Sykora write:

> As schools, or school districts adopt these standards, it would be prudent to give time for educators to review and plan for implementation. It would be important for educators to take a step-by-step approach to adoption and implementation of standards, perhaps setting a goal of working on one or two standards at a time to feel comfortable and successful, before taking on additional standards. These standards and examples can be used to support educators, students, school leaders, policy makers, funders, and also a springboard for future researchers to further empirically examine educational standards for educational leaders, and technology specialists. (Compton & Sykora, 2021)

Standards are part of the Structural frame; they are concrete and actionable competencies, goals, and frameworks. They are a needed initial step in adoption and change. But change also requires a cultural shift, an emotional buy-in. That lens of organizational change is the Symbolic frame.

Building a Culture of Ritual and Ceremony

Another gap that Sykora sees in digital citizenship practice is around emotions and culture, saying, "I think that a lot of times digital citizenship isn't a priority of a system or if it is, it can be very much sort of fear-based . . . it could be that teachers may not feel confidence and competence in digital citizenship." According to Sykora, this means that educators may be lacking a "natural connection to digital citizenship" (interview, September 2021).

One way to forge that natural connection and alleviate fears is through the Symbolic frame practice of rituals and ceremonies. These activities help create a positive and united, rather than fear-based, culture. In Lee G. Bolman and Terrence E. Deal's book *Reframing the Path to School Leadership: A Guide for Teachers and Principals*, the authors write, "The lag between instruction and outcomes often makes teachers' full impact on students visible only years later . . . Faith and confidence, kindled by familiar cultural symbols rather than immediate tangible outcomes confirmed by data, help define a good school" (Bolman & Deal, 2019). The teaching of digital citizenship is preventative education, and it's hard to see what you prevented from ever happening. Yes, you can track data on cyberbullying incidents or assessments on digital citizenship, but with such a broad subject, it's hard to visibly see outcomes. This can be dispiriting for educators, but adding ritual and ceremony can motivate and build that confidence.

"Ceremony is a core aspect of culture," write Bolman and Deal. "It serves as a theatrical stage for dramatizing values, recognizing heroes and heroines, and telling stories" (Bolman & Deal, 2019). Here are some examples of rituals and ceremonies where digital citizenship can be added:

- STEM events
- Media Literacy Week
- Digital Citizenship Week
- literacy events
- Red Ribbon Week
- parent/teacher events

Culture can also be communicated through displays, speech, and stories. This can mean honoring student achievements. Those honors can go beyond grades, such as an award for kindness. Positive social media stories about students or the school community can be shared. And the emphasis in these stories and displays should be on the accomplishments, the yeses, the positives—not just the fear and nos. Instead of signs about the dangers of cyberbullying, consider a sign that says exactly how many students *don't* cyberbully. Instead of a poster telling what *not* to do digital etiquette-wise, consider one that focus on what they *should* do. For example, some things to showcase could be:

- signage in the school library saying, "We check multiple sources for the facts!"
- display in a classroom of positive Post-it notes
- poster in a computer lab that reads, "Do the right thing, even if no one is looking!"
- displays and signs that emphasize a growth mindset such as "I like to challenge myself!" or "I can persevere, even when times are tough!"

As you reflect and consider ways to improve and build on your school culture, ask yourself these questions:

- How are we displaying our school's values?
- How are we communicating those values to our school community?
- What stories are we telling about digital citizenship?
- Are we rewarding and recognizing good digital behavior? Or are we just punishing the bad?

Teaching Digital Citizenship Across Grade Levels

Before many of today's children are even born, they have an online presence. Their name and even an ultrasound picture may be posted online. Baby shower registries for them are posted and shared, starting a lifelong practice of sharing personal data with companies. They are digital citizens before they are citizens. Despite this, digital citizenship instruction may not begin before middle school, and a student may have their first phone or social media account before they have any formal instruction on the topic. So when should the teaching start? Sykora suggests, "I think with all of the standards, the beginning age-appropriate time is as young as kindergartners. Kindergartners are also exposed to the digital world before they get to school" (interview, September 2021).

Because research around the use of technology for PK–2 students is still somewhat limited, educators may find fewer resources for children at this level. (See the "Teaching digital citizenship to early learners" sidebar for ideas to consider for younger learners.) The ISTE Standards for Students include age-band articulation of the standards grouped into ages 4–7, 8–11, and 12–14, which can be a guide for teaching across grade levels, including early learners (ISTE, 2016). In addition, another resource for teaching digital citizenship is ISTE Connect, a professional learning network with a Digital Citizenship forum where educators can share and swap ideas on digital citizenship. There are many educators doing innovative and unique work for young learners in their own classroom. While these educators may not have written an article or created a training, they have information to share.

ISTE CONNECT

Also important to consider, as discussed in Chapter 5, is inclusivity for learners of different abilities, as students at different ages and developmental stages may learn these concepts in different ways. Age and ability do not always go hand in hand, so educators need to make adaptations to be able to meet the needs of all the students in their classroom. The ISTE Educator Leader Standard 2.2.b recommends that educators "advocate for equitable access to educational technology, digital content and learning opportunities to meet the diverse needs of all students."

When thinking about teaching digital citizenship across ages, consider two factors: what's developmentally appropriate and which platforms and devices they are using. My staff and I survey media use among the elementary students we teach digital citizenship to. From our surveys, we found using YouTube and gaming to be the most popular activities. Common Sense Media found similar stats when conducting a Common Sense Census in 2020 with ages zero to eight. They write that "online videos now dominate children's screen time," and found that approximately 37% of that video watching came from YouTube or other online videos. Gaming was the second most popular online activity in this age cohort, comprising 16% of their daily use (Rideout & Robb, 2020).

> When thinking about teaching digital citizenship across ages, consider two factors: what's developmentally appropriate and which platforms and devices they are using.

> # TEACHING DIGITAL CITIZENSHIP TO EARLY LEARNERS
>
> My staff and I have taught thousands of kindergartners through second grade students digital citizenship topics. What we've learned is:
>
> - **Shorten the lessons.** Plan for a 15–25 minute lesson for the younger students. They have shorter attention spans. The rest of the time have it focused on activities, coloring, movement, and so on.
> - **Add movement.** Try to incorporate more movement and tactile activities into teaching these students. For example, when teaching about asking permission to use devices, we play a game of "Mother May I?" to illustrate asking permission and getting permission to act.
> - **Cover online safety less.** In general, students these ages aren't on social media and are lacking the digital literacy skills and the access to devices to type/text strangers. Focus on different digital concepts to teach, such as digital literacy, and start defining what's public versus private information.

Teach your students where they're at. When talking to elementary students, use examples of gaming or YouTube rather than apps like Snapchat. Talking about screen time using an online video as an example would be more relatable to them. When working with secondary students, by contrast, focus on the positive aspects of digital citizenship, such as creating, collaborating, and the power of technology. Also, understand that adolescents use social media more than younger children, so digital communication and online safety principles come to the forefront. Secondary students are also looking ahead past high school, applying for jobs online or looking at colleges. Having college- and career-centric discussions with high school students is more relevant to them and their future.

Based on our teaching experiences, Table 7.3 offers recommendations of topics to focus on for each grade level.

TABLE 7.3 Digital Citizenship Topics Across K–12

GRADE LEVEL	TOPIC			
K–2	• asking permission • basic vocabulary media literacy concepts			
3–5	all K–2 topics	• digital footprint • how to evaluate media • using the internet for positive purposes		
6–9	all K–2 topics	all 3–5 topics	• basics of algorithms • digital economy • bias in media • digital communication • cyberbullying	
10–12	all K–2 topics	all 3–5 topics	all 6–9 topics	• applying for jobs and colleges online • digital identities • healthy online relationships

Teaching digital citizenship goes beyond high school, of course. Career professionals, such as teachers, can use more education. But by teaching across these ages and developing those foundational skills, educators can better prepare their students. "Ensuring that they're starting young is giving exposure to these concepts," says Sykora. "This way of being online gets built over time. So, it really is a fully academic career practice" (interview, September 2021).

Planning for Digital Citizenship

Digital citizenship is a concept and a standard that's built into multiple subjects across grades K–12. Integrating it can seem daunting, but with proactive planning the task can be more easily divided and conquered. One form of planning is through a scope and sequence document. This kind of visual planning document can help organize curriculum. The term "scope" is the breadth and depth of the content and skills related to the curriculum. "Sequence" is the word that describes how the skills and content are both ordered and presented to students over a period of time. There's a wide variability in creating a scope and sequence. They can go into more or less detail. They can be created for just a week, or an entire calendar year. A scope and sequence can focus on specific grade levels or concepts. See the appendix for a Sample Scope of Sequence for teaching digital citizenship to kindergarten through second grade.

Another way to plan for digital citizenship is to look at a calendar. See what holidays, national "day ofs," and other celebrations are occurring through the school year. This way of planning incorporates the Symbolic frame and uses rituals and ceremonies for learning digital citizenship. Here are some suggestions of digital citizenship-related days through the school year (National Today, 2022):

- January: Data Privacy Day, New Year's Day
- February: Safe Internet Day, Clean Out Your Computer Day
- March: World Compliment Day, National Day of Unplugging
- April: World Health Day, National School Librarian Day
- May: World Password Day, National Creativity Day
- September: National Video Games Day, Citizenship Day
- October: UNESCO Media Literacy Week, Digital Citizenship Week
- November: National STEM/STEAM Day, World Kindness Day

By adding digital citizenship to existing celebrations around the school or district, educators can save time and effort. They also can get more buy-in through tying digital citizenship to existing activities. Using some of those digital citizenship-related days, a simple scope and sequence for planning could look like Table 7.4.

TABLE 7.4 Sample 4th Grade Digital Citizenship Scope and Sequence for Q3

MONTH	ISTE STUDENT STANDARD INDICATOR	TIE-IN DAY	SUGGESTED ACTIVITY
January	1.1.a. Students articulate and set personal learning goals, develop strategies leveraging technology to achieve them and reflect on the learning process itself to improve learning outcomes.	New Year's Day	Create digital goals to achieve for the year (i.e. learning a new digital tool, or finding a healthy balance of online activities).
February	1.2.b. Students engage in positive, safe, legal and ethical behavior when using technology, including social interactions online or when using networked devices.	Safe Internet Day	Discuss ways to be safe when talking to others online. Share examples of positive and kind online behavior.

Whatever planning tool is used, by incorporating standards, whether ISTE standards, state standards, or others, educators can make sure their activities are in alignment with their goals and can carry their knowledge of standards into their practice. School leaders can also assist in these planning tools by providing time for educators, input on school celebrations, and a budget throughout the year dedicated to these ceremonies and rituals.

Chapter Wrap-Up

It's easier to make a rule than follow it—especially when you're the one having to follow it. Hopefully, this book has given you helpful strategies on making those rules that account for the realities of being a teacher in a classroom, while including everyone in the conversation. As we've explored throughout this book, achieving change must include all stakeholders, and applying different frameworks and being open to viewing this complex topic through different lenses can aid in that work.

The Appendix offers more strategies and suggestions to develop your digital citizenship policies and deepen your practice. Just remember: Ultimately, the best strategy is the one that works for your school or district. Good luck.

Conclusion

Implementing change is hard. In Chapter 6, I (Carrie) shared a little of my story of being a target of a coordinated campaign because of my attempt to implement a new approach to digital citizenship education. I admit, the stress from that experience still makes my heart beat a little faster every time I walk up the Capitol steps. Trying something new means not only refining logistics, marketing, and scaling, but also changing attitudes. In my experience, it's far easier to develop a process for implementation than it is to shift values and culture.

Yet despite the difficulty, it's worth it. I see those efforts with myself, our state board of education, and other education leaders moving the needle: I don't hear the term "online safety" as much as I did just a few years ago. This suggests a shift in attitudes from one of fear to a measure of acceptance that the internet is continually with us and how to adapt. Schools in my state, particularly in some rural areas, are contacting my company Digital Respons-Ability looking for more digital citizenship resources. There's also more awareness of the issue from elected officials, with a push for more coordination and funding. I am encouraged by the changes I've been seeing when it comes to the digital citizenship. More voices are bringing attention to such issues as privacy, digital wellness, security, and media literacy, and these topics are being addressed at local, regional, and international levels.

How to Approach Digital Citizenship, by Role

How will you make change in your work? Every school community role has an opportunity to shift attitudes, and even culture, in their area. Because everyone in a school community is busy, I encourage you to focus on whatever situation or topic you're dealing with. As you go, spend some time in the Appendix exploring examples and ideas—and scan the QR code to check out more resources and guides on this book's companion site.

COMPANION SITE

Now, let's dive into how to address this topic, no matter what your role.

Classroom Teachers

Teachers have a big impact on an individual student level. They're the ones that may be able to see some of these digital citizenship cultural changes up close. Unlike a school leader, a teacher can more easily see change through conversations, grades, reactions, and behavior. These important lenses can inform policy making at all levels of an organization.

Classroom teachers have a vital perspective that can inform policy and implementation. To learn more about how you can be involved, review the sections of Chapter 2 about how internal partnerships provide ways that teachers can be part of larger schoolwide initiatives.

Coaches and Coordinators

According to the ISTE Standards for Coaches, instructional technology coaches are "change agents." This means those in coaching and related coordinator positions are tasked with cultivating and shifting culture around digital citizenship. These highly specialized positions are up on the research and best practices and have largely removed the term "online safety" from their vocabulary.

Being a coach can sometimes be frustrating. These individuals may have the vision for a desired destination, but that doesn't mean others are lining up to follow. Patience and communication are needed, and the suggestions for having hard conversations and community engagement in Chapter 6 can help coaches convey their digital citizenship vision more broadly.

State or District Education Leaders

State and district leaders have a bird's-eye, top-level approach to change. This perspective allows them to look beyond their organization and see trends and new practices, as well as to see how local, state, and national laws may influence their schools. It also means that they need those school roles, including teachers and coaches, on the ground to more accurately understand changes and make sure all parts of the school community are included.

The first part of this book, Chapters 1-3, is the most relevant to school leaders. But school leaders should read the second part, particularly Chapters 5 and 7, so that they can better understand what it's like for teachers and students in individual classrooms.

School Community Leaders

Many school community leaders care about the topic of digital citizenship, but don't know what to do about it. Digital citizenship is a broad topic with many involved, which means for external partners and leaders, there's not one person or place to contact. These community leaders may be able to help the school reach its larger digital citizenship goals, but they are often underutilized and left out of conversations that could be meaningful.

For school leaders wanting to be involved, reading Chapter 1 and the process of policy design can offer a better understanding of how schools address issues. They will also find guidance in Chapter 2 on how external partnerships can be created and utilized in the school community.

Reflection and Moving Forward

Another way I recommend using this book is as a chance to sit back and self-reflect. Where are you in your digital citizenship journey? What are you trying to accomplish? As you're working to make change, you'll need to shift values and attitudes towards digital citizenship. You'll get pushback and the question "Why?" So make sure you can answer that question. What is your "why?" There are conversation starters and self-reflective questions sprinkled throughout the chapters, as well as the companion site. And if you want a deeper dive into this topic, check out the references at the end of the book.

If you're wondering where to start, look closer at the ISTE Standards that appear throughout the book. The ISTE Standards are a wonderful guide to help answer your "why" and assist with a more standardized implementation of digital citizenship. Throughout my scaling and implementation journey, I've found them to be a good starting point, as they can help educators and coaches come to consensus on definitions and with curriculum development.

Perhaps you're in a similar spot as I was years ago. You recognize digital citizenship is important, but want to move it beyond the occasional classroom lesson or Digital Citizenship Week. You want to shift the culture and approach to digital citizenship to match the modern realities of technology in our lives. You want to make change, but you're not sure where to start, or how to do it. This book is for anyone, from those at the beginning of their digital citizenship journey to those who have been doing the work for years. No matter who you are in education, we all have a role to play in digital citizenship. All of us are needed to shift the culture and systems. All of us can make change.

Appendix

This appendix includes resources, templates, policies, and more to help you and your organization create best practices and policies in digital citizenship. For more downloadable resources, see this book's companion site: deepeningdigitalcitizenship.org.

COMPANION SITE

Part I Resources

Part I resources include system-level examples of artifacts, guidance, and supports to infuse digital citizenship across district efforts—from board leadership to policy development.

Board Member Documentation Example

The following example is an L.A. Unified Board Resolution, which provides system-level directives for senior district leaders. (Scan the QR code to view.) In this particular example, a board member calls for increased digital citizenship supports and was the first directive provided in the district.

SAMPLE BOARD RESOLUTION

This example can serve to support your system-level efforts for board leadership language and concepts. Additionally, this language provides guidance on how to frame the creation of a task force comprising various stakeholders to inform digital citizenship implementation efforts. In this example, you will also find a directive to establish and engage in Digital Citizenship Week.

"Digital Presence with Purpose" Digital Footprint Guidance

The following framing and guidance provide a launching point to help you create a professional learning experience for school leaders to reflect on their own digital footprint.

- Invite participants to use a search engine and use the following search query format, entering their name in quotations and a unique but well-known identifier for them, such as their alma mater or school site they work in:
  - "[NAME]" [COLLEGE or SCHOOL SITE]
  - e.g., "Vanessa Monterosa" Harvard

- Using quotation marks is an important component of the search query to ensure that the full name is searched as one unit. Participants with common names may need to consider particularly unique identifiers, such as hobbies or other activities or locations associated with them.

- Instruct participants to review search page results as well as image results.

- Use the following guiding questions to support participants in reviewing their digital footprint:
  - **Strengths:** What parts of your current digital presence demonstrate your education leader identity?
  - **Opportunities:** What parts of your current digital presence do you want to continue to amplify/build?
  - **Gaps:** What parts of your identity as an education leader are missing from your digital footprint?
  - **Considerations:** What current digital elements exist that might compromise your digital footprint as an education leader?
- Give participants 10 minutes to explore and react to their findings.
- Invite participants to share their discoveries. Participants will find they are not the only ones surprised by their existing digital footprint.

Responsible Use Policy Example

For an example of a responsible use policy, scan the QR code to view a version of L.A. Unified's policy, which was developed and designed alongside stakeholder feedback.

Focus groups were held to capture student, school staff, and family feedback to ensure this high-profile policy was accessible and easy to understand. More importantly, educators requested it be written in a way to serve as an instructional tool and guide when discussing digital citizenship.

RESPONSIBLE USE POLICY

Social Media Policy for Employees Example

For an example of a social media policy for employees, scan the QR code to view a version of L.A. Unified's policy, which was updated to create opportunities around leveraging social media for teaching and learning.

SOCIAL MEDIA POLICY FOR EMPLOYEES

Social Media Policy for Students Example

For an example of a social media policy for students, scan the QR code to view a version of L.A. Unified's policy, which was the first policy I drafted to support an aspirational instructional vision of a 1:1 program.

SOCIAL MEDIA POLICY FOR STUDENTS

Part II Resources

Part II of this book puts policy into practice. Included in this part of the appendix are documents that can help you create best practices, such as sample marketing emails, a needs assessment, a scope and sequence, and a sample lesson plan.

Sample Emails to Market Digital Citizenship

Creating change requires the entire school community. The following is a sample email with text that could be used to involve your school community in digital citizenship conversations.

FOR AN EVENT

SUBJECT: You're Invited: Conversation about Digital Citizenship

Dear Community Member,

Digital citizenship is the ethical and responsible use of technology—and it's an issue that affects us all. Please join us for a FREE virtual event to discuss strategies for teaching at school and home on this topic.

We are holding a virtual event with _____ to talk about how we can all keep students safe and responsible online. Please attend this FREE event and offer your input so we can know how we can help our school community.

A link to register for the event is on the flyer and below: [ADD LINK]

We value you as a partner in our school community. All ages are welcome at the event so please share with friends and family. We hope you can join us and share your voice.

Sincerely,
XX

(Attach a PDF of your digital flyer with a hyperlink.)

FOR A SURVEY

SUBJECT: We need your input!

Dear Community Member,

With more remote learning and technology use than ever, our students need to understand how to safely and competently navigate the digital world. We want to hear from YOU about the best ways to do that. We are soliciting feedback on how our school can improve digital citizenship education. Please help us help your students with this important topic.

Take this survey [TIME FRAME][ADD LINK] and let us know how we can better keep students safe and responsible online.

We appreciate your input and perspective. We value you as a partner in our school community. Please take the survey by _____.

Thank you,
XX

FOR A NEW RESOURCE

SUBJECT: New free resource for our school community

Dear Community Member,

With more remote learning and technology use than ever, our students need to understand how to safely and competently navigate the digital world. That's why we created _____ to assist teachers and families. This resource contains [DESCRIPTION].

Please share with your family, children, and friends. Also, check out these resources on digital citizenship: [LIST ADDITIONAL RESOURCES].

We value you as a partner in our school community. Please let us know what else we can do to help.

Warmly,
XX

Sample Digital Citizenship Needs Assessment

To understand the different knowledge levels, concerns, and priorities around digital citizenship in your school community, consider creating a needs assessment. A needs assessment is a process used to help improve organizations, and can help determine what the potential barriers are that hold the organization back from reaching its goals. A well-crafted and executed needs assessment clarifies the problem so more informed decisions are made.

> There are a variety of ways to conduct a needs assessment. When deciding the method, consider the budget, timeline, and how much feedback is needed.

When planning a needs assessment, determine who will conduct it, as well as what schools, sites, and individuals will be involved. For digital citizenship, some members of the school community that may want to be involved include:

- teachers
- parents
- law enforcement such as school resource officers
- school counselors
- school media specialists
- after school program leaders
- principals
- students
- nonprofit leaders
- elected officials such as state legislators or council members

There are a variety of ways to conduct a needs assessment. When deciding the method, consider the budget, timeline, and how much feedback is needed. Do you want to survey a smaller group of people in depth? Or would you rather cast a wider net with more responses?

The following is a basic sample needs assessment around digital citizenship that could be adapted for different communities (CDC, 2013). The best method for conducting this sample needs assessment would be as an individual interview face-to-face or over the phone/virtual conferencing.

WHERE ARE YOU AT?	What do you know about digital citizenship?	What do your students/children/colleagues know about digital citizenship?
WHERE DO YOU WANT TO GO?	What do you want to know about digital citizenship?	What do you think students/children/colleagues should know about digital citizenship?
WHAT CAUSES THE PROBLEM?	What are problems around the topic of digital citizenship?	What do you think is causing these problems?
WHAT ARE POTENTIAL SOLUTIONS TO THE PROBLEM(S)?	What do you think should be done to solve any problems around digital citizenship?	Are there other groups/individuals that should be included in the solution?
WHAT ARE THE FEELINGS ABOUT THE PROBLEM(S)?	How do you feel about digital citizenship?	How do your students/children/colleagues feel about digital citizenship?

After a needs assessment is completed, it needs to be evaluated. Consider evaluating feedback through the Four Frames Theory (Bolman & Deal, 2021). As discussed throughout this book, individuals have different frames through which they see the same issue. By categorizing feedback into one of the four frames, you can better understand where people are coming from.

PROBLEM	CAUSES	HOW TO SOLVE?	PRIORITY TO ADDRESS?	WHICH FRAME?
Not enough digital citizenship education	Not enough time to teach digital citizenship	Provide more staff time to teach	High	Structural

Sample Scope and Sequence

There are different ways to create a scope and sequence. This one uses digital citizenship categories spread out over four quarters of the school year. But educators can also create their own month to month or week to week, on different digital citizenship topics or grade levels—or even based upon books like in an English Language Arts course.

Elementary Grades K-2 Scope and Sequence

GRADE	ISTE STANDARD/ LEARNING GOAL	Q1	Q2	Q3	Q4
Kindergarten	1.2.b With guidance from an educator, students understand how to be careful when using devices.	Demonstrate how to turn devices on and off, as well as why they need to be restarted and shut down.	Recognize how devices need power/batteries and demonstrate how to charge them.	Discuss the importance of asking permission to use someone's device.	Explain how devices can be fragile and illustrate how to hold one properly.
First Grade	1.2.c. With guidance from an educator, students learn about ownership and sharing the work of others.	Compare and contrast the difference between public and private property.	Describe the concept of copyright and provide examples of copyrighted items.	Differentiate between copyrighted property and ones that are free to use.	Recommend ways to ask permission using real-life and digital examples, then have the students role play asking.
Second Grade	1.2.a. Students practice responsible use of technology through teacher-guided online activities and interactions to understand how the digital space impacts their life (ISTE, 2016).	Draw and discuss activities/hobbies that are done online and those that are done in person.	Define what a password is. Explain why a password is important. With the students, create strong passwords. and passphrases.	Lecture on the concept of online privacy and how it relates to online safety. Differentiate what is public versus what is private online.	Demonstrate how to logon to a platform step by step. Define vocabulary terms in that process such as "login," "username," and "submit."

What's Your Social Media Platform?

Digital etiquette is not just about knowing what to say online but also where to say it. In this activity, have the students select what social media platforms they would use for each of the following tasks. As long as students can make an argument about why they would use that platform for that specific task, there are no wrong answers.

- staying in contact with your friends at school
- staying in contact with a friend who has moved away
- staying in contact with grandparents
- figuring out what you want to do on your next vacation
- sharing pictures from your trip with your friends
- letting other people know about your hobbies
- looking for a book for your book club
- researching a place you might want a job at
- asking for help on a homework question
- getting ideas for a science fair project
- showing off your Halloween costume
- meeting new people who have similar interests
- catching the news
- finding out new things about your favorite TV show
- keeping your parents in the loop
- figuring out how you want to decorate your room
- figuring out which hairstyle would work best for you
- letting people know that you have gotten accepted to college
- letting your friends know about a service project that you are helping run
- planning a surprise party for one of your friends

References

Ahn, J., Bivona, L. K., & DiScala, J. (2011). Social media access in K-12 schools: Intractable policy controversies in an evolving world. *Proceedings of the American Society for Information Science and Technology, 48*(1), 1-10. https://doi.org/10.1002/meet.2011.14504801044

American Association of School Librarians [AASL]. (2021, January 11). *Home*. National School Library Standards. https://standards.aasl.org

Appel, M., Marker, C., & Gnambs, T. (2019). Are social media ruining our lives? A review of meta-analytic evidence. *Review of General Psychology, 24*(1), 60-74. https://doi.org/10.1177/1089268019880891

Argyle, M., Salter, V., Nicholson, H., Williams, M., & Burgess, P. (1970). The communication of inferior and superior attitudes by verbal and non-verbal signals. *British Journal of Social and Clinical Psychology, 9*(3), 222-231. https://doi.org/10.1111/j.2044-8260.1970.tb00668.x

Askari, E., Brandon, D., Galvin, S., & Greenhow, C. (2018). Youth, learning and social media in K-12 education: The state of the field. In J. Kay and R. Luckin (Eds.), *Rethinking learning in the digital age: Making the learning sciences count, 13th International Conference of the Learning Sciences (ICLS)* (344-351). International Society of the Learning Sciences. https://repository.isls.org//handle/1/764

Assistant Secretary for Public Affairs [ASPA]. (2021, September 10). *LGBTQI+ youth*. StopBullying.gov. https://www.stopbullying.gov/bullying/lgbtq

Atske, S., & Perrin, A. (2021, September 10). *Home broadband adoption, computer ownership vary by race, ethnicity in the U.S.* Pew Research Center. https://www.pewresearch.org/fact-tank/2021/07/16/home-broadband-adoption-computer-ownership-vary-by-race-ethnicity-in-the-u-s

Auxier, B., Anderson, M., Perrin, A., & Turner, E. (2020, July 28). *Parenting children in the age of screens*. Pew Research Center. https://www.pewresearch.org/internet/2020/07/28/parenting-children-in-the-age-of-screens

Becker, S. P., Breaux, R., Cusick, C. N., Dvorsky, M. R., Marsh, N. P., Sciberras, E., & Langberg, J. M. (2020, October 14). Remote learning during COVID-19: Examining school practices, service continuation, and difficulties for adolescents with and without attention-deficit/hyperactivity disorder. *Journal of Adolescent Health, 67*(6), 769-777. https://doi.org/10.1016/j.jadohealth.2020.09.002

Bolman, L. G., & Deal, T. E. (2013). *Reframing organizations: Artistry, choice, and leadership* (5th ed.). Jossey-Bass.

Bolman, L. G., & Deal, T. E. (2019). *Reframing the path to school leadership: A guide for teachers and principals* (3rd ed.). Corwin.

Bolman, L. G., & Deal, T. E. (2021). *Reframing organizations: Artistry, choice, and leadership* (7th ed.). Jossey-Bass.

Boursier, V., Musetti, A., Gioia, F., Flayelle, M., Billieux, J., & Schimmenti, A. (2021). Is watching TV series an adaptive coping strategy during the COVID-19 pandemic? Insights from an Italian community sample. *Frontiers in Psychiatry, 12*. https://doi.org/10.3389/fpsyt.2021.599859

Bowles, N. (2018, October 26). The digital gap between rich and poor kids is not what we expected. *The New York Times*. https://www.nytimes.com/2018/10/26/style/digital-divide-screens-schools.html?action=click&module=RelatedLinks&pgtype=Article

Boyd, D. (2008). Why youth (heart) social network sites: The role of networked publics in teenage social life. In D. Buckingham (Ed.), *Youth, identity, and digital media*. MIT Press. https://ssrn.com/abstract=1518924

Boyd, D. (2014). *It's complicated: The social lives of networked teens*. Yale University Press.

Brewer, G., & Kerslake, J. (2015, July). Cyberbullying, self-esteem, empathy and loneliness. *Computers in Human Behavior, 48*, 255–60. https://doi.org/10.1016/j.chb.2015.01.073

Building the Field of Community Engagement. (2014). *Distinguish your work: Outreach or community engagement? An assessment tool*. https://nexuscp.org/wp-content/uploads/2015/02/BTF-DistinguishYourWork.pdf

CAST (2018). *Universal Design for Learning Guidelines*. http://udlguidelines.cast.org

Centers for Disease Control and Prevention. [CDC]. (2013). *Community needs assessment*. https://www.cdc.gov/globalhealth/healthprotection/fetp/training_modules/15/community-needs_fg_final_09252013.pdf

Centers for Disease Control and Prevention [CDC]. (2020, March 2). *Risk and protective factors: Violence prevention*. https://www.cdc.gov/violenceprevention/youthviolence/riskprotectivefactors.html

Choi, M. (2016). A concept analysis of digital citizenship for democratic citizenship education in the internet age. *Theory and Research in Social Education, 44*, 565–607. https://doi.org/10.1080/00933104.2016.1210549

Choi, M., Glassman, M., & Cristol, D. (2017). What it means to be a citizen in the internet age: Development of a reliable and valid digital citizenship scale. *Computers & Education, 107*, 100–112. https://doi.org/10.1016/j.compedu.2017.01.002

The Church of Jesus Christ of Latter-day Saints. (2021a). *General Authority quotes on technology*. https://tech.churchofjesuschrist.org/wiki/General_Authority_quotes_on_technology

The Church of Jesus Christ of Latter-day Saints. (2021b). *Message from the First Presidency and quorum of the twelve apostles*. https://www.churchofjesuschrist.org/study/manual/missionary-standards-for-disciples-of-jesus-christ/message-from-the-first-presidency?lang=eng

Coburn, C. E., & Penuel, W. R. (2016). Research–practice partnerships in education: Outcomes, dynamics, and open questions. *Educational Researcher, 45*(1), 48–54. https://doi.org/10.3102/0013189X16631750

Cohen, C. J., & Kahne, J. (2012). *Participatory politics: New media and youth political action*. MacArthur Foundation.

Common Sense Education. (n.d.). Common Sense Education Recognition Program. https://www.commonsense.org/education/recognition-program

Common Sense Education. (2022). Digital Citizenship Week. https://www.commonsense.org/education/digital-citizenship-week

Consortium of School Networking [CoSN]. (2013, March). *Rethinking acceptable use policies to enable digital learning: A guide for school districts.* https://practices.learningaccelerator.org/artifacts/cosn-rethinking-acceptable-use-policies-to-enable-digital-learning-a-guide-for-school-districts

Crompton, H. (2018). *Education reimagined: Leading systemwide change with the ISTE Standards.* International Society for Technology in Education.

Crompton, H., & Sykora, C. (2021). Developing instructional technology standards for educators: A design-based research study. *Computers and Education Open, 2.* https://doi.org/10.1016/j.caeo.2021.100044

Culp, K., Honey, M., & Mandinach, E. (2005). A retrospective on twenty years of education technology policy. *Journal of Educational Computing Research, 32*(3), 279–307.

Digital Respons-Ability. (2022, October 26). *Parent's guide to gaming and ADHD.* https://respons-ability.net/parents-guide-to-gaming-and-adhd

Gleason, B., & Von Gillern, S. (2018). Digital Citizenship with Social Media: Participatory practices of teaching and learning in secondary education. *Journal of Educational Technology & Society, 21*(1), 200–212.

Gottman, J. M., & Gottman, J. S. (2015). Gottman couple therapy. In A. S. Gurman, J. L. Lebow, & D. K. Snyder (Eds.), *Clinical handbook of couple therapy* (5th ed., 129–157). Guilford Press.

Greenhow, C., Staudt Willet, K. B., & Galvin, S. (2021). Inquiring tweets want to know: #Edchat supports for #RemoteTeaching during COVID 19. *British Journal of Educational Technology, 52*(4), 1434–1454. https://doi.org/10.1111%2Fbjet.13097

Haddock, J. N., & Hagopian, L. P. (2020). Suicidality and self-harm in autism spectrum conditions. In S. W. White, B. B. Maddox, & C. A. Mazefsky (Eds.), *The Oxford handbook of autism and co-occurring psychiatric conditions* (348–368). Oxford University Press. https://doi.org/10.1093/oxfordhb/9780190910761.013.18

Hiatt, J. (2006). *ADKAR: A model for change in business, government, and our community.* Prosci.

International Society for Technology in Education [ISTE]. (2016). *ISTE Standards for Students.* https://www.iste.org/standards/for-students

International Society for Technology in Education [ISTE]. (2017). *ISTE Standards for Educators.* https://www.iste.org/standards/iste-standards-for-teachers

International Society for Technology in Education [ISTE]. (2018). *ISTE Standards for Education Leaders.* https://iste.org/standards/iste-standards-for-education-leaders

International Society for Technology in Education [ISTE]. (2020). *ISTE Standards for Coaches.* https://www.iste.org/standards/iste-standards-for-coaches

International Society for Technology in Education [ISTE]. (2020). *DigCit Commit.* https://digcitcommit.org

Ito, M., Sims, C., Perkel D., Mahendron, D., & Finn, M. (2009). *Hanging out, messing around, and geeking out: Kids living and learning with new media.* MIT Press.

James, C., Weinstein, E., & Mendoza, K. (2019). *Teaching digital citizens in today's world: Research and insights behind the Common Sense K–12 digital citizenship curriculum.* Common Sense Media.

Jenkins, H. (2009). *Confronting the challenges of participatory culture: Media education for the 21st century.* MIT Press.

Johannes, N., Vuorre, M., & Przybylski, A. K. (2021). Video game play is positively correlated with well-being. *Royal Society Open Science*, 8(2). https://doi.org/10.1098/rsos.202049

Johnson, C., & Dempsey, L. (2020, November 11). How Coronavirus might have changed TV viewing habits for good. *The Conversation*. https://theconversation.com/how-coronavirus-might-have-changed-tv-viewing-habits-for-good-new-research-146040

Kellner, D., & Share, J. (2005). Toward critical media literacy: Core concepts, debates, organizations, and policy. *Discourse: Studies in the Cultural Politics of Education*, 26(3), 369–386. https://doi.org/10.1080/01596300500200169

Kirby, A. (2021, August 26). Is there a link between neurodiversity and mental health? *Psychology Today*. https://www.psychologytoday.com/us/blog/pathways-progress/202108/is-there-link-between-neurodiversity-and-mental-health

Kokina, A., & Kern, L. (2010). Social story interventions for students with autism spectrum disorders: A meta-analysis. *Journal of Autism and Developmental Disorders*, 40, 812–826. https://doi.org/10.1007/s10803-009-0931-0

Kowert, R., Domahidi, E., & Quandt, T. (2014). The relationship between online video game involvement and gaming-related friendships among emotionally sensitive individuals. *Cyberpsychology, Behavior, and Social Networking*, 17(7), 447–453. https://doi.org/10.1089/cyber.2013.0656

Leitner, Y. (2014). The co-occurrence of autism and attention deficit hyperactivity disorder in children—what do we know? *Frontiers in Human Neuroscience*, 8, 268. https://doi.org/10.3389/fnhum.2014.00268

Lickteig, M. K. (2004). Brand-name schools: The deceptive lure of corporate-school partnerships. *The Educational Forum*, 68(1), 44–51. https://doi.org/10.1080/00131720308984602

Literat, I. (2014). Measuring new media literacies: Towards the development of a comprehensive assessment tool. *Journal of Media Literacy Education*, 6(1), 15–27. http://dx.doi.org/10.23860/jmle-6-1-2

Livingstone, S., & Stoilova, M. (2021). *The impact of digital experiences on adolescents with mental health vulnerabilities*. Parenting for a Digital Future. https://blogs.lse.ac.uk/parenting4digitalfuture/2021/12/15/adolescents-mental-health

Mani, A., Mullainathan, S., Shafir, E., & Zhao, J. (2013). Poverty impedes cognitive function. *Science*, 341(6149), 976–980. https://doi.org/10.1126/science.1238041

Martinelli, K. (2021). *Why do kids have trouble with transitions?* Child Mind Institute. https://childmind.org/article/why-do-kids-have-trouble-with-transitions

Marx, T. (2020, April 22). *Plan and deliver: Educating students with disabilities in remote settings*. REL Midwest. https://ies.ed.gov/ncee/edlabs/regions/midwest/blogs/students-disabilities-remote-settings.aspx

Misawa, M. (2010). Queer race pedagogy for educators in higher education: Dealing with power dynamics and positionality of LGBTQ students of color. *International Journal of Critical Pedagogy*, 3(1), 26–35. http://libjournal.uncg.edu/ijcp/article/view/68

Monterosa, V. (2015). Developing digital citizenship. *Leadership*, 44(3), 30–32.

Monterosa, V. (2017). *Digital citizenship district-wide: Examining the organizational evolution of an initiative* (Publication No. 10286695) [Doctoral dissertation, California State University – Long Beach]. ProQuest.

Monterosa, V. (2020, August 4). *An educator's guide to cultivating a digital presence with purpose*. Latinos for Education. https://www.latinosforeducation.org/2020/08/04/digital-presence-with-purpose

Monterosa, V. (2021, January). Digital citizenship for education leaders. *Leadership Magazine*. https://leadership.acsa.org/digital-citizenship-for-education-leaders

Morrell, E. (2002). Toward a critical pedagogy of popular culture: Literacy development among urban youth. *Journal of Adolescent & Adult Literacy, 46*(1), 72–77. https://www.jstor.org/stable/40017507

Morris, A., & Anthes, E. (2021, August 23). For some college students, remote learning is a game changer. *The New York Times*. https://www.nytimes.com/2021/08/23/health/covid-college-disabilities-students.html?smid=url-share

Mossberger, K., Tolbert, C. J., & McNeal, R. S. (2008). *Digital citizenship: The internet, society, and participation*. MIT Press. https://doi.org/10.7551/mitpress/7428.001.0001

Mullin, J. (2021, December 26). 2021 was the year lawmakers tried to regulate online speech. *Electronic Frontier Foundation*. https://www.eff.org/deeplinks/2021/12/2021-was-year-lawmakers-tried-regulate-online-speech

National Center on Disability and Journalism [NCDJ]. (2022). *Disability Language Style Guide*. https://ncdj.org/style-guide

National Today. (2022, January 13). *National Holiday Calendar*. https://nationaltoday.com/national-day-calendar

Nerenberg, J. (2021). *Divergent mind: Thriving in a world that wasn't designed for you*. HarperOne.

New York State Education Department. [NYSED]. (2021). *Computer science and digital fluency*. http://www.nysed.gov/curriculum-instruction/computer-science-and-digital-fluency

Ortutay, B., & Klepper, D. (2021, October 5). Facebook whistleblower testifies: Five highlights. *AP News*. https://apnews.com/article/facebook-frances-haugen-congress-testimony-af86188337d25b179153b973754b71a4

Payne, R. K. (2013). *A framework for understanding poverty: A cognitive approach* (5th ed.). aha! Process.

Penuel, W. R., & Gallagher, D. J. (2017). *Creating Research Practice Partnerships in Education*. Harvard Education Press.

Pinker, S. (2014). *The sense of style: The thinking person's guide to writing in the 21st century*. Viking Books.

Rafalow, M. H. (2020). *Digital divisions: How schools create inequality in the tech era*. University of Chicago Press.

Ribble, M., & Park, M. (2019). *The Digital citizenship handbook for school leaders*. International Society for Technology in Education.

Rideout, V., & Robb, M. B. (2020). *The Common Sense census: Media use by kids age zero to eight, 2020*. Common Sense Media. https://doi.org/10.3886/ICPSR37491.v2

Rogers-Whitehead, C. (2018a, June 14). 4 things to know about teaching digital literacy to refugees. ISTE. https://www.iste.org/explore/Digital-citizenship/4-things-to-know-about-teaching-digital-literacy-to-refugees

Rogers-Whitehead, C, (2018b). *Teaching digital citizenship to students who are refugees.* Rowman & Littlefield.

Rogers-Whitehead, C. (2020). *Serving teens and adults on the autism spectrum: A guide for libraries.* Libraries Unlimited.

Rogers-Whitehead, C. (2021). *The 3 Ms of fearless digital parenting: Proven tools to help you raise smart and savvy online kids.* Skyhorse Publishing.

Rubia, K. (2018). Cognitive neuroscience of attention deficit hyperactivity disorder (ADHD) and its clinical translation. *Frontiers in Human Neuroscience, 12,* 100. https://doi.org/10.3389/fnhum.2018.00100

Sánchez Abril, P., Levin, A., & Del Riego, A. (2012). Blurred boundaries: Social media privacy and the 21st century employee. *American Business Law Journal, 49*(1), 63-124. https://ssrn.com/abstract=2004438

Sanders, M. G. (2005). *Building school-community partnerships: Collaboration for student success.* Corwin Press.

Singer, N. (2013). They loved your G.P.A. Then they saw your tweets. *The New York Times.* http://www.nytimes.com/2013/11/10/business/they-loved-your-gpa-then-they-saw-your-tweets.html

Soep, E. (2014). *Participatory politics: Next-generation tactics to remake public spheres.* MIT Press.

Starks, A. (2021, September 22). The promise of schools as digital citizenship hubs. *Connected Learning Alliance.* https://clalliance.org/blog/the-promise-of-schools-as-digital-citizenship-hubs

Tekinbaş, K. S., Jagannath, K., Lyngs, U., & Slovák, P. (2021). Designing for youth-centered moderation and community governance in Minecraft. ACM *Transactions on Computer-Human Interaction, 28*(4), 1-41. https://doi.org/10.1145/3450290

Timmerman, M. C., & Schreuder, P. R. (2014). Sexual abuse of children and youth in residential care: An international review. *Aggression and Violent Behavior, 19*(6), 715-720. https://doi.org/10.1016/j.avb.2014.09.001

Tynes, B., & Monterosa, V. (2014). The making of a global citizen: A model of supporting civic learning opportunities among urban Latino youth. In E. Middaugh & B. Kirshner (Eds.), *#YouthAction: Becoming political in the digital age* (169-189). Information Age Publishing.

U.S. Department of Health and Human Services. (2017). *Report to Congress: Young adults and transitioning youth with autism spectrum disorder.* https://www.hhs.gov/sites/default/files/2017AutismReport.pdf

Utah House of Representatives. (2020, May 8). Jon Hawkins. http://house.utah.gov/rep/HAWKIJ

Utah State Legislature. (2021). *Digital Wellness, Citizenship, and Safe Technology Commission 2021.* https://le.utah.gov/committee/committee.jsp?year=2021&com=SPEDCS

Vogels, E. A. (2021, September 10). *Digital divide persists even as Americans with lower incomes make gains in tech adoption.* Pew Research Center. https://www.pewresearch.org/fact-tank/2021/06/22/digital-divide-persists-even-as-americans-with-lower-incomes-make-gains-in-tech-adoption

Watkins, S. C., & Cho, A. (2018). *The digital edge: How Black and Latino youth navigate digital inequality.* New York University Press.

Index

A

AASL (American Association of School Librarians), 120
ABC-CLIO, 82
Ability, ADKAR Change Management, 13
abortion, "fishbowl conversation," 96
Acceptable Use Policy, 5
ACSA (Association for California School Administrators), 32
ADHD (attention deficit hyperactivity disorder), 71, 73-74, 77
ADKAR Model for change management, 10, 13-14, 37, 47, 98. *See also* change
Ahn, Bivona, & DiScala, 6
anxiety disorder, 72, 77, 88
Appel et al., 81
Apple products, Guided Access, 86
Argyle et al., 87
Askari, Brandon, Galvin, & Greenhow, 6
ASPA, 61
assessment, doing, 28
assumptions, confronting, 61
Autism After 21, 71
autism spectrum disorder, 74, 82, 84
Awareness, ADKAR Change Management, 13, 37
awareness, creating, 47

B

Becker et al., 73
biases, confronting, 61
binge-watching TV, 72, 74
blocking websites, 102
board members, working with, 27
Board Resolution example, 130
Bolman & Deal
 ceremony, 122
 elected officials, 108
 empathy and values, 59
 needs assessment, 135
 partnerships, 23, 31
 policy design, 16
 professional learning, 40
 QR code for Four-Frame Model, 10
 Structural frame, 99
 Symbolic frame, 53

Boursier et al., 72
Bowles, 57
Boyd, 5, 41
Brewer & Kerslake, 89
Building the Field of Community Engagement, 106
bullying, 74. *See also* cyberbullying

C

calendar, planning "day ofs," 127
caregivers and parents, roles of, 101
CAST, 83
CDC (Centers for Disease Control and Prevention), 88, 135
Center for Humane Technology, 80
ceremony and ritual, building culture of, 122-123
change. *See also* ADKAR Change Management
 developing skills for, 116
 training for, 47-48
child pornography, 24
Choi, 33-34
Choi, Glassman, & Cristol, 33-34
The Church of Jesus Christ of Latter-day Saints, 57-58
Citizen, ISTE Standards for Educators, 113
classroom teachers, 140
Clinical Psychological Science, 80-81
coaches and coordinators, 140
Coaches section, ISTE Standards, 58
coalition-building, 108-109
Coburn & Penuel, 33
"cognitive inflexibility," 84
cognitive resources, 55-56
Cohen & Kahne, 5, 18
collaboration
 and coherence, 26
 between departments, 27
 results, 25
comic book stories, creating, 89
Common Sense Education, 20-22
Common Sense Media, 7, 26, 80, 124
Common Sense Recognition Program, 36
communicating. *See also* digital communication; nonverbal communication; teamwork and social skills
 finding ways of, 63-65
 teamwork and social skills, 86

communication and neurodiversity, 69–71
communities. *See also* school community leaders
   conversations, 104
   including in policy design, 103
   surveying, 104
companion site, xiii, 104, 140
Computers & Education, 121
Computers in Human Behavior, 88–89
confidence and competency, building, 61
Connected Learners, ISTE Standards for Education Leaders, 15, 44, 113. *See also* personalized learning
conversations, managing, 96–102
coordinators and coaches, 140
coping methods, 72
COPPA (Children's Online Privacy Protection Act), 115
corporations, partnering with, 29–30
counseling leads, working with, 26
COVID-19 pandemic, 20, 22, 38, 72–73
Crompton, 47
Crompton & Sykora, 121
cross-collaborations, 8–9
Culp, Honey, & Mandinach, 6
culture
   basing on ritual and ceremony, 122–123
   definitions, 16
"Curse of Knowledge," 61. *See also* knowledge
cyberbullying, 7, 29, 41, 61, 75. *See also* bullying
Cyberpsychology, Behavior and Social Networking, 76

D

DCW (Digital Citizenship Week), 20–22, 30–31
decision makers, identifying, 27
depression, neurodiverse students, 88
Designer, ISTE Standards for Educators, 69
Desire, ADKAR Change Management, 13
diagnostic tools, 79
difficult conversations, managing, 96–102
#DigCit policy. *See also* policies
   cross-collaborations, 8–9
   designing, 6–8
#DigCitCommit congress, 48
DigCitCommit initiative, 118
#DigCitLeaders. *See also* leadership
   cultivating, 36–39
   developing, 41–44
   interactive-session design, 45–47
   Twitter posts, 37
digital access, 55
Digital Citizen Advocate standard, 58

Digital Citizen, ISTE Standards for Students, 113
digital citizenship
   age of students, 20
   building coalitions, 94
   conceptualizing, 17–18
   definition discussion, 45, 63
   definitions and conceptualizations, 7
   dissertation research, 5
   faith and beliefs, 57–63
   framing, 7
   goal of, 93
   Google Search trends, 64
   in ISTE Standards for Educators, 112
   ISTE Standards for Students, 120–122
   memorializing efforts, 32
   navigating politics of, 92–95
   perception of, 44
   planning for, 127–128
   planning strategies, 26–27
   scaling, 102–107
   scope and sequence, 128
   state and national standards, 118–120
   system-level gaps, 5–6
   teaching, 118–122
   teaching across grade levels, 123–126
   teaching at state hospital, 77–79
   teaching to early learners, 125
   topics across K–12, 126
   views and priorities, 59
Digital Citizenship and Wellness Commission, 107
Digital Citizenship Handbook for School Leaders, 36
Digital Citizenship Week, QR code, 14
digital communication, 87. *See also* communicating
digital dilemma activity, 45
digital empathy, teaching, 88–89. *See also* empathy
digital etiquette, teaching, 89
digital footprint analysis, 46
digital parenting classes, teaching, 96–97. *See also* parents and caregivers
Digital Presence Framework
   development, 37
   overview, 38–39
   reviewing, 46
"Digital Presence with Purpose," 37, 42–45, 47, 130–131
digital wellness concepts, teaching, 85
disabilities. *See* neurodivergent students
discussions, engaging in, 28
disinformation, politics of, 92
distractions, limiting, 86

district education leaders, 141
district policy discussion, 45-46. *See also* policies
distrust, 55
doomscrolling, 74
dopamine functions, 74-75

E

ECS (Education Commission of the States), 114
educators. *See also* ISTE Standards for Educators
   hesitancy of, 39
   and neurodivergent students, 82-83
elected officials, working with, 107-110
elementary students, 124
emails, samples for marketing, 132-133
emoji, 87, 89
emotional resources, 55-56
empathy, building, 59-60. *See also* digital empathy
Empowered Learner, ISTE Standards for Students, 113
Empowering Leader, ISTE Standards for Education Leaders, 15, 41, 54, 61, 69, 79-80. *See also* leadership
engagement, 104-107
Equity and Citizenship Advocate, ISTE Standards for Education Leaders, 15, 95
etiquette, teaching, 89
events, marketing via email, 132
evidence, sharing, 38-39
Example Participant Tweet, 47
executive functioning, 74-75, 78
external leaders, partnering with, 28-30

F

Facebook
   "Get Digital" resource, 31
   impact on vulnerable people, 80
facility leads, working with, 26
Fidget Activity Book, 85
filtering websites, 102
focus groups, 104
forums and facilitators, 104
Four-Frame Model
   evaluating feedback, 135
   Human Resources, 11-12, 40-41, 117
   and key roles, 108
   as multi-frame tool, 12
   Political, 11-12, 23-24, 108
   QR code, 10-12
   Structural, 11-12, 40-41, 99, 108, 116, 122
   Symbolic, 11-12, 16, 59, 108, 117, 122
Frontiers in Psychiatry, 72

G

Gainsford, Rick, 102-103, 118
gameplay, positive side of, 76
gap analysis, 104. *See also* system-level gaps
"Get Digital" resource, 31
Gleason & Von Gillern, 5
Global Collaborator
   ISTE Standards for Students, 54, 61-62
goals, clarity and achievability of, 98
Google Search trends, 2021, 64
Gottman, John, 97
Gray, Carol, 89
Greenhow, Staudt Willet, & Galvin, 38
groups, size of, 86
Gudmundson, Tay, 71, 76
Guided Access, Apple, 86

H

Haddock & Hagopian, 84
Haugen, Frances, 80
Hawkins, Jon, 107, 109
Hiatt
   awareness stage, 37
   goals, 98
   goals for change, 13
   professional learning, 41
   training for change, 47
hospital, teaching digital citizenship at, 77-79
Human Resources frame, Four-Frame Model, 11-12, 40-41, 117

I

identify-first language, 70
identity, examining, 60-62
implementation strategies, 114-117
incentives, providing, 114, 121
instructional leads, working with, 27
interactive session, 45-47
internal leaders, partnering with, 25-27. *See also* leadership
intervention, applying to difficult conversations, 97-102
ISTE Connect, 124
ISTE Standards
   clarification of definitions, 64
   Digital Citizen Advocate, 58
   and NYSED (New Your State Education Department), 119

ISTE Standards for Education Leaders. *See also* leadership
  Connected Learner, 15, 44, 113
  Empowering Leader, 15, 41, 54, 61, 69, 79-80
  Equity and Citizenship Advocate, 15, 95
  QR codes, xii, 10
  Systems Designer, 15, 25, 95, 109
  use of technology, 42
  Visionary Planner, 15-16, 44, 94-95, 101
ISTE Standards for Educators. *See also* educators
  Citizen, 113
  Designer, 69
  digital citizenship, 112
  Leader, 113
  QR code, xii
ISTE Standards for Students. *See also* students
  age-band articulation, 124
  Digital Citizen, 113
  digital citizenship, 120-122
  Empowered Learner, 113
  Global Collaborator, 54, 61-62
  QR code, xii
IT leads, working with, 26-27

J

James, Weinstein, & Mendoza, 45
Jenkins, 5, 18, 45
Johannes et al., 76
Johnson & Dempsey, 72
Journal of Adolescent Health, 73

K

K-2, sample scope and sequence, 136
K-12, topics across, 126
Kellner & Share, 5, 18
kindergartners, 123, 125
Kirby, 74
knowledge. *See also* "Curse of Knowledge"
  ADKAR Change Management, 13
  resources and evidence sharing, 38
Kokina & Kern, 89
Kowert et al., 76
KQED, partnership with, 47-48

L

L.A. Unified
  Board Resolution, 130
  legal department, 17
  "Now Matters Later," 24
  social media task force, 4-5
language barriers, 55
Lapus, Merve, 7, 26
laws
  and policies, 117
  providing guidance and support on, 115
LDS (Latter-day Saints), 57-58
Leader, ISTE Standards for Educators, 113
leadership. *See* #DigCitLeaders; Empowering Leader; internal leaders; ISTE Standards for Education Leaders; organizational leadership
legal representative, working with, 27
library story time, 52-53
listening and observation, encouraging, 89
Literat, 33-34
Livingstone & Stoilova, 26
LSTA (Library Services and Technology Act) grant, 68

M

Mani, 56
marginalized groups, 55, 66
marketing, 104-107, 132-133
Martinell, 84
Martinez, Sumiko, 70-71
McDonald, Caitlin, 96, 99, 103
media literacy, 18
meetings, scheduling bimonthly, 27
mental health leads, working with, 26
mental illness, technology use, 80-82
Minecraft Education Edition, 34
Misawa, 60
Monterosa
  #DigCit policy, 6
  Digital Presence Framework, 38
  dissertation research, 5, 9
  interactive session, 45
  thought leadership, 32
Mormon church, 57-58
Morrell, 18
Morris & Anthes, 73
Mullin, 102

N

national and state standards, 118-120
National School Library Standards, 120
National Today, 127
NCDJ (National Center on Disability and Journalism), 70
needs assessment, 104, 134-135
Nerenberg, Jenara, 70
"Netiquette" performance, 22
neurodivergent students
  across grade levels, 124
  digital-citizenship skills, 83
  risk factors, 74-75
  teaching, 68-69, 74
neurodiversity and communication, 69-71
nonprofits, partnering with, 29
nonverbal communication, 86-87
"Now What?" 99
NYSED (New York State Education Department), 118-119

O

observation and listening, encouraging, 89
online engagement, 43
online safety vs. online learning, 116
organizational leadership. *See also* leadership
  Four-Frame Model, 10
  ISTE Standards for Education Leaders, 10
  overview of frameworks, 9-10
  Prosci ADKAR Model, 10
Ortuary & Klepper, 80
outreach, 104-107

P

PACT Act, 101
pain point, identifying, 99-102
pandemic, 20, 22, 38, 72-73
parents and caregivers, roles of, 101. *See also* digital parenting classes
partnerships
  aligning, 25
  extending opportunities, 30-34
  external leaders, 28-30
  with internal leaders, 25-27
  inviting, 47-48
  leveraging, 22-23
  organizational approach, 23-25
  research practice, 33-34
  school site leaders, 22
  thought leadership, 32-33
  varieties, 20
Payne, 55
Penuel & Gallagher, 33
people-first language, 70
perceptions, identifying, 60
personalized learning, 64. *See also* Connected Learners
perspectives, considering, 53-56
Pew Research
  digital access, 55
  parenting, 101
Pinker, Steven, 61
PK-2 students, 124
policies. *See also* #DigCit policy; district policy discussion
  Acceptable Use Policy, 5
  and laws, 117
  purpose and benefits, 17
  Responsible Use Policy, 7
  revisiting and updating, 8
policy design
  considerations, 5
  organizational approach, 16-17
  participatory practice, 7-8
Political frame, Four-Frame Model, 11-12, 23-24, 108
politics of digital citizenship, navigating, 92-95
positionality, concept of, 60
poverty culture, 55
privacy concerns, 18
professional learning
  cultivating #DigCitLeaders, 38
  and online engagement, 43
  organizational leadership, 40-41
Prosci ADKAR Model for change management, 10, 13-14, 37, 47, 98. *See also* change

Q

QR codes. *See also* resources
  Acceptable Use Policy, 5
  Autism After 21, 71
  Common Sense Recognition Program, 36
  Companion Site, xiii, 104, 140
  DigCitCommit initiative, 118
  #DigCitLeaders Twitter Posts, 37
  Digital Citizenship District-Wide, 9
  Digital Citizenship Handbook for School Leaders, 36
  Digital Citizenship Week, 14
  Education Leader Standards, xii
  Educator Standards, xii
  Example Participant Tweet, 47
  Fidget Activity Book, 85

Four-Frame Model, 10
"Get Digital" resource, 31
ISTE Connect, 124
ISTE Standards for Education Leaders, 10
Minecraft Education Edition, 34
National School Library Standards, 120
Prosci ADKAR Model, 10
Responsible Use Policy, 131
Sample Board Resolution, 130
Serving Teens and Adults on the Autism Spectrum, 82
Social Media Policy for Employees, 131
Social Media Policy for Students, 132
Student Standards, xii
Student-Led Performance about "Netiquette," 22
Teaching Digital Literacy to Refugees, 56
Teenage Celebrities at Digital Citizenship Week, 21
Tips for Hosting a Digital Parenting Event, 97
Tools for School Leaders, 61
UDL Guidelines, 83
quarterly goals, determining, 27

R

Rafalow, 5, 47
Reframing the Path to School Leadership: A Guide for Teachers and Principals, 122
refugees, teaching, 56-57
Reinforcement, ADKAR Change Management, 13
remote learning, 73
resources. *See also* QR codes
　marketing via email, 133
　providing, 115
　scarcity of, 23
　sharing, 38
Responsible Use Policy, 7, 131
ritual and ceremony, building culture of, 122-123
Rogers-Whitehead, 57, 77, 82
Rosenthal, Michael, 84
RPPs (research-practice partnerships), 33-34
Rubia, 74, 77

S

Salt Lake Community College, 56
Sánchez, Levin, & Del Riego, 6
school community leaders, 141. *See also* communities
school leaders
　as thought leaders, 109-110
　tools for, 61
screen time, talking about, 85
self-reflection, 61
self-regulation and transitions, 84-86

sensory activities, including, 85
Serving Teens and Adults on the Autism Spectrum, 82
sexting, dangers of, 24
shared language, finding, 63-65
sharing knowledge, resources, and evidence, 38-39
Silicon Valley, digital gap, 57
Singer, 41
skills, developing for change, 116
Snapchat, 24
social media
　Congressional intervention, 101
　and COVID-19 pandemic, 38
　as instructional opportunity, 42-43
　platforms, 137
Social Media Policy for Employees, 131
Social Media Policy for Students, 132
social media task force, L.A. Unified, 4-5
social skills and teamwork, 86-89
Soep, 5, 18
stakeholders
　coalitions, 23-24
　identifying decision makers, 27
　including in policy design, 7-8, 103-104
　professional learning, 41
　students, 41
standards
　applying to programs, 115
　and Structural frame, 122
Starks, 101
state and national standards, 118-120
state education leaders, 141
state hospital, teaching digital citizenship at, 77-79
Steyer, Jim, 80
strategy, focusing on, 41
stress, relieving, 72
Structural frame, Four-Frame Model, 11-12, 40-41, 99, 108, 116, 122
students. *See also* ISTE Standards for Students
　roles in developing policies, 54
　as stakeholders, 41
support, providing, 115
surveys, marketing via email, 133
SWOT (Strengths, Weaknesses, Opportunities, Threats), 46
Sykora, Carolyn, 64, 121-123, 126
Symbolic frame, Four-Frame Model, 11-12, 16, 59, 108, 117, 122
system-level gaps, 5-6, 9. *See also* gap analysis
Systems Designer, ISTE Standards for Education Leaders, 15, 25, 95, 109

T

teaching digital literacy to refugees, 56
teamwork and social skills, 86-89. *See also* communicating; nonverbal communication
technological innovation, resistance to, 6
technology
   effect on young people, 81
   equitable access to, 124
   and mental health, 80-82
   people of varying abilities, 71-76
   as scapegoat, 82
   using with neurodivergent individuals, 68-69
Tekinbas, Jagannath, Lyngs, & Slovák, 34
thought leadership, 32-33
Timmerman, 77
tips for hosting a digital parenting event, 97
tools for school leaders, 61
transitions and self-regulation, 84-86
transportation issues, 55
trust, building, 114-115
TV, binge-watching, 72, 74
Twenge, Jean, 80
Twitter, 37, 47
Tynes & Monterosa, 5

U

UDL (Universal Design for Learning), 83
UEN (Utah Education Network), 102
U.S. Department of Health and Human Services, 74, 88
USBE (Utah State Board of Education), 102
Utah, navigating politics in, 92-95
Utah State Hospital, 77

V

values
   emphasis in Symbolic frame, 16-17
   identifying, 60
video gaming, 76
video watching, 124
virtual spaces, 76
Visionary Planner, ISTE Standards for Education Leaders, 15, 44, 94-95, 101
von Zastrow, Claus, 114-115, 117, 121

W

Watkins & Cho, 47
websites, filtering and blocking, 102
"What do you see?" 96-97
"What do you think?" 99-102
What? Why? How? When? 100
"What's in it for me?" 40-41
"What's in it for you?" 40-41

Y

youth in custody, teaching, 65-66
YouTube, 81, 104, 124-125

www.ingramcontent.com/pod-product-compliance
Lightning Source LLC
Chambersburg PA
CBHW081448070526
44586CB00019B/2267